The Silence of the Hams

A Casting Director's Pictorial Memoir
Casting the greatest comedians of all time!

By Craig Campobasso

Copyright © 2020 by Craig Campobasso

All rights reserved. No part of this publication may be reproduced, distributed, or transmitted in any form or by any means, including photocopying, recording, or other electronic or mechanical methods, without the prior written permission of the publisher, except in the case of brief quotations embodied in critical reviews and certain other noncommercial uses permitted by copyright law. For permission requests, write to the publisher, addressed "Attention: Permissions Coordinator," at the address below.

Film Classics Press
A Division of Micro Publishing Media, Inc

PO Box 1522
Stockbridge, MA 01262
www.micropublishingmedia.com
info@micropublishingmedia.com
Ordering Information:
Quantity sales. Special discounts are available on quantity purchases by corporations, associations, and others. For details, contact the publisher at the address above.

ISBN 978-1-944068-96-7

Printed in the United States of America

The Silence of the Hams: A Pictorial Memoir

A Tribute to the 1994 Cult Classic Parody of *The Silence of the Lambs* and *Psycho*.

Celebrating the 25th Anniversary

Books by Craig Campobasso

The Autobiography of an ExtraTerrestrial Saga

Book One: I AM Thyron
Book Two: Waking Thyron
Book Three: Thyron's Dossier
Book Four: The Huroid Revolution and Other Warring Creatures

The Extraterrestrial Species Almanac:
The Ultimate Guide to Greys, Reptilians, Hybrids, and Nordics

TABLE OF CONTENTS

Dedication	8
Introduction	9-12
Foreword	13-15
Film Synopsis	16
Lead Cast	17-21
Supporting Cast	22-31
Pre-Production	32-35
Casting Memories	36-39
Actors we Couldn't Find Roles for	40-43
Production	44-97
Mel Brooks: The King of Comedy	98-99
Sets	100-104
Funny Faces and Behind-the-Scenes Antics	105-115
Famous People who Visited our Set	116-117
It's a Wrap	118-119
San Remo Restaurant	120-127
Phyllis Diller: The Queen of Comedy	128-132

Production Stills	133-138
Italian Press Junket	139-154
Blu-ray Rerelease 2020	155-158
Parting Oinks	159-162
About the Author	163-164
Ham Articles	165-166
Epilogue	167-168
In Memoriam	169

Dedication

For my mother, Marie Donna King Campobasso, who was the *Ham's* mascot. She lived near our production office and visited us often. Being the casting director I made sure I put her in the film. She loved it. I got my gregarious personality from her. She kept Dom DeLuise in stitches on the set too. Ezio loved her. Everyone loved her. I loved her most for always believing in me even before I believed in myself.

I would also like to cast my net out to the entire cast and crew who made this movie possible. We all got inducted into the Hambone Hall of Hilarity and our fond memories live on.

INTRODUCTION

In late February 1993 I got a call to meet on a movie called *The Silence of the Hams* as their potential casting director. All I was told is that it was a spoof of *Silence of the Lambs* and *Psycho*. Being a fan of Mel Brooks movies since childhood, and the *Airplane* movies, I loved that style of comedy and jumped at the chance to meet Italian funnyman Ezio Greggio, the film's star, director, writer and producer. I was hired on the spot and the fun and silly antics began. When Ezio and I first met we were like long lost brothers, mischievously anticipating pranks to pull on each other. Our friendship remains to this day, twenty-five years later.

I sent out a breakdown to all agents and managers on March 10, 1993 detailing the roles available for submission. I made my usual star-name lists for the lead roles (names they could afford in their budget) and went over the list with Ezio and producer Julie Corman.

For the role of Doctor Animal we considered Jerry Lewis, Jack Palance, Joe Pesci, Paul Rubens, Sid Caesar and George Carlin. I had worked with Dom DeLuise on Steven Spielberg's *Amazing Stories* in the mid-80s along with Burt Reynolds and Loni Anderson. Although we had initially thought of Dom for the role of Pete Putrid, when that went to comedian Stuart Pankin it was like a light went off in all our heads: Dom DeLuise for Doctor Animal. I made him and offer, called him to talk about the role, set his deal, and hired his sons David and Peter in smaller roles.

Names in consideration for Jo Dee Fostar were Ryan O'Neill, Steve Guttenberg, John Ritter, Charles Rocket and Woody Harrelson. But I wanted Billy Zane. I knew he had great comedic timing. Ezio was dead set against it. He said, "You mean the guy from Dead Calm. He only plays heavy's." I told Ezio that we could make Zane an offer based on a creative meeting. If after the meeting, Ezio didn't like Billy for the role, he could back out of the offer. He finally caved in and Ezio took that meeting with Billy at his apartment on North Rossmore in Hollywood. Afterwards, he realized that Billy was just as zaney (pun intended) as the rest of us. I quickly closed Billy's deal at CAA with agent Jane Berliner. Honestly, I don't think anyone else could have played it better. The same goes for Dom DeLuise's Doctor Animal.

We made an offer to Teri Garr (*Young Frankenstein*) for the role of Jane, but she passed. Others we considered for Jane were Rosanna Arquette, Nora Dunn, Christina Applegate and Rebecca De Mornay. I had brought Charlene Tilton in for a cameo role. I told Charlene to oblige me; I knew Ezio would fall in love with her when he met her, and I would let it be his idea to cast Charlene as Jane. We needed to cast that role like yesterday. Charlene may be pint sized, but the talent and vivaciousness that oozes from her is infectious. My rouse worked and Charlene became our Jane at long last, the last of the lead cast to be signed.

I also made an offer to Mimi Rogers (*Austin Powers* and Tom Cruise's first wife) for the role of Lily, but that went south as well. We ultimately fell in love with and hired Joanna Pacula, who had recently starred in *Tombstone* with Kurt Russell.

I was in heavy negotiations with Martin Balsam's agent to reprise and spoof his role in *Psycho*. It was not looking well. Others we considered were Rodney Dangerfield, Buddy Ebsen, Norman Fell, Sherman Hemsley, Edward James Olmos, Peter Boyle, Don Rinkles, Paul Bartel and Arte Johnson. I ultimately closed the deal and Martin Balsam was set to play Detective Martin Balsam. Ezio and I celebrated that day; adding an Academy Award winner to our cast.

The Ranger role went to John Astin. We had considered Tommy Chong, John Byner, Jerry Stiller, Tom Poston, James Callahan, Telly Savalas and Michael Constantine. But John's sense of comedic timing and delivery, not to mention he was Gomez Addams in *The Addams Family*, won us over.

To play opposite Ezio (Antonio Motel) we considered these actresses for his mother: Katherine Helmond, Polly Holliday, Lainie Kazan, and Lu Leonard. In talking with agent Jack Gilardi at ICM he encouraged me to make an offer to Shelley Winters. She accepted and I closed her deal. My mother Marie was a huge Shelley Winters fan. I brought Mom to the set to meet Shelley. In this stage of her life, Shelley was befuddled most of the time and seemed disoriented. She would even forget who I was. When I tried to introduce my mother to her on location, she said "Who are you again?" I replied "Craig Campobasso, the casting director." "Oh that's right," she replied. "My agent says I have to be nice to you." She walked away never acknowledging Mom. But I think her mind was focused on preparing for her next scene. Needless to say, we had Shelley Winters, another Oscar winner (twice) in our cast. That was something to ogle over. Mom was so happy to have seen her in person; it made her day.

For Olaf we considered Tommy Davidson, Doug E. Doug, Flex, Eddie Griffin and Sinbad. But Ezio and I were *Police Academy* fans. Bubba Smith climbed onboard the *Hams* star-train to play the Finnish man of mystery.

I wanted Phyllis Diller for the part of Mr. Laurel's (Rip Taylor) secretary really bad, even though we were considering Anne Haney, June Allyson, Marion Ross, Billie Bird and Ann B. Davis. I made an inquiry to Diller's manager Milt Suchin about her possible interest and fee. (I'm mean, really. What do you pay an icon?) I brought the idea to Julie Corman, our producer, and Ezio, who had final say. He did not know who Ms. Diller was, so he nixed the idea. Julie and I kept telling him how famous she was, a comedic genius, and what a coo it would be to have her in the film. For goodness sake, she starred in Bob Hope road pictures! He still refused. So I had to be honest with her manager. Milt called Phyllis and they would come to the office to meet Ezio. I waited until the last minute to tell Ezio they were coming for fear of him refusing the meeting.

Phyllis and Milt arrived that afternoon and the entire staff was tongue-tied, awestruck, and floating on clouds. Phyllis Diller's infectious aura of light and laughter made every mouth grin wider than it had ever before. Phyllis brought a box of her standup gigs and movies on VHS and she said to Ezio, "Let me show you some Phyllis Diller," and then finished with that famous cackle of hers that could have been insured for a million dollars like Betty Grables legs. We all sat there and laughed until our stomachs hurt. Ezio guffawed too. But after she left, he still did not want to hire her, wanting to save money on the role. (Her price was extremely fair.) In the following days, Julie and I and the office staff shamed him into hiring the living legend. Finally he gave in begrudgingly. So I hurriedly closed her deal for fear he might change his mind.

During the shoot Ezio fell in love with Phyllis Diller. (Who wouldn't?) After post production, Ezio shared with me that when he was screening the movie for distributors in Europe, their jaws literally fell open—one remarking: "Ezio! How in the world did you get Phyllis Diller in your movie? This is unbelievable!" (I'm sure Phyllis helped seal the deal for distribution.) When Ezio next visited Los Angeles, he got down on bended knees before me, bowed three times, and thanked me profusely for hounding him to hire Phyllis Diller. He became her number one fan right after me.

For the role of Mr. Laurel we considered Norman Fell, Henry Jones, Art Carney and Jerry Stiller, but made an offer that was accepted by the flamboyant and funny confetti thrower Rip Taylor.

I hired comedic legend Larry Storch to play the Sergeant. Storch only ever referred to me as Spaceman. Finally one day I asked him why he called me Spaceman. He replied looking to the heavens, "Because you are a Spaceman." Storch must be a time-traveler, because in 2011 I released my first book *The Autobiography of an ExtraTerrestrial Saga: I AM Thyron*. There are four books released to date in the series and in the end there will be seven volumes.

Producer Corman suggested she had contacts with directors John Carpenter (*Halloween*) and Joe Dante (*Gremlins*) for cameos. She called Carpenter directly, and I made an offer to Joe Dante, whom I had previously worked with on *Amazing Stories*. They both accepted. I suggested John Landis (*An American Werewolf in London* and *Thriller*), made him an offer, and he accepted. Not long after John wrapped, he thanked me in a kind letter.

I began physical casting at the Lantana Center in Santa Monica, our temporary office space, on March 17, 1993. Word got around town fast as I cast more and more star names, and agents were begging me to consider their star names for any roles available, even a cameo or walk-on role.

At the beginning of April we moved into our permanent location, a soundstage with offices attached in Sun Valley, California. James Newport, our production designer, built the inside of the *Psycho* house here, as well as Doctor Animal's (Dom DeLuise ala Hannibal Lechter) jail cell, and Jo Dee Fostar's (Billy Zane) apartment. Jacques Haitkin was our director of photography whose recent works include *Venom* and *Black Panther*.

Before the film's release Jodie Foster's team contacted Ezio and wanted him to screen the film for her. She wanted to make sure there were no bad humor jokes. Ezio graciously obliged, and she gave him her blessing.

Ezio wanted Roger Moore's picture to hang on the wall in Jo Dee Fostar's apartment. Production contacted Moore's reps, and Moore graciously agreed.

Here we are at the 25th anniversary of the film's release. It's become a cult classic and will soon be rereleased on Blu-ray with interviews from Ezio Greggio, Julie Corman, Billy Zane, Charlene Tilton, Lance Kinsey, myself and more. Ezio, Billy, Charlene, and I also did commentary for the Blu-ray, where we watched and talked about the film for the first time since its 1994 release.

During the production, I took more than a thousand pictures and decided to create this pictorial book and production stories for the fans. These were some of the happiest memories I've ever had on a film production in my three decades of casting film and television, with over 100 projects under my casting belt.

Sit back, relax, and get your smile on, for you are about to enter into the world of the most ridiculous, funniest comedians of our time. Stark. Raving. Comedy. Just like the poster promises.

I'll leave you with my favorite bit in the movie that Dom DeLuise created on the spot while filming. Doctor Animal said to Jo Dee Fostar, "Iggy-boo." Jo replied with furrowed brows, "Iggy-Boo. What is that?" Doctor Animal: "It's my happy noise."

May you make lots of happy noises looking through this pictorial memoir as I share some of the highlights and set stories from the production of *The Silence of the Hams*.

Keep Smiling,

Craig Campobasso

FOREWORD

I'M MR. SILENCE OF THE HAMS, FOREVER

by Ezio Greggio

To whom it may concern:

The first man that said, "I have a dream" was not Obama, but me, Ezio Greggio, when I saw *Psycho* for the first time in a drive-in theater: it was December 23 in Finland, I was in a convertible car, it was a little chilly. I was only 12 years old, and my dream was to "make a spoof movie out of this masterpiece." I said the same thing on the radio when I saw *The Silence of the Lambs* and again the exact same phrase for the other 139 movies I saw. We have spoofed all of those movies in THE SILENCE OF THE HAMS. This movie is the most hilarious, crazy, outrageous, sophisticated, awarded, surprising, loved, astonishing, dreamy, unbelievable, sexy, horrifying, smelly, hilarious, sedative, un-understandable, laggard, irreverent, religious, innovative, what-the-hell, politically incorrect, two fettuccine Bolognese, one coffee, check please…

S.O.T.H is all of the above and much more. I know people who saw my movie 20 or 30 times (yes I can confirm, they're either in a nuthouse, or they are very forgetful, or they are drunkards) and every time they see it again, they discover a new quote in it from the movies spoofed in *S.O.T.H*. Even today, after every screening people go straight to their lawyers and file a lawsuit against me, but I don't care: everybody has a different way of showing me their admiration.

My casting director, Craig (Calogero in Italian) Campobasso (coincidently the same name of a city in Italy, but they are not relatives) and I did an unbelievable job. If you read the list of actors we had in the movie you'd probably think we deserve an Honorary Academy Award for the Best Cast Ensemble in Movie History: Dom DeLuise, Billy Zane, Martin Balsam playing the same role of the detective he did in Hitchcock's *Psycho*, Shelley Winters, Joanna Pacula, Charlene Tilton, John Astin, Larry Storch, Rip Taylor,

Bubba Smith, Phyllis Diller, John Landis, John Carpenter, Joe Dante, Stuart Pankin, Henry Silva, Eddie Deezen, Peter and David DeLuise, Al Ruscio, Rudy De Luca and a cameo from the legendary Mel Brooks himself.

I'm honored to have worked with Academy Award-winning actors, but also with Giuseppe Cianciafico from the craft service department. He did the worse poisoned cheeseburgers in movie history: half of the crew is still in hospital 25 years later…Fucking Giuseppe… anyway…

The movie was distributed in more than 50 Countries and had many media talking about it: sometimes in movie magazines but most of the time in missing objects columns and obituary announcements.

Out of all the memorable scenes I have directed and acted in, there is one that I will never, ever forget. It will stay with me for the rest of my life. It was the one when I… when I… sorry I forgot.

I received many awards around the world throughout my career. I also got an Oscar during the ceremony at the Chinese Theater, but not for long: the guards saw me when I took the statue from the table and into my tuxedo, so I had to give it back. Too bad. And too heavy: my inside pocket broke, and I had to throw my tuxedo away. S@#t!

I've done over 40 movies in my career, but *Silence of the Hams* is the one I love the most, and it will always be in my heart. And in my liver, guts, foot phalanx, and my ass.

Ezio Greggio
Actor- Screenplayer – Director – Producer – Driver and Fan of *Silence of the Hams*

Ezio Greggio and Craig Campobasso on set.

The Film

SYNOPSIS

Billy Zane plays Jo De Fostar, an FBI agent assigned to a serial/psycho killer case. Fostar finds himself meeting with incarcerated Doctor Animal (Dom DeLuise ala Hannibal Lechter) to enlist his help to put an end to the killers killing spree. Fostar's girlfriend Jane (Charlene Tilton) works for Laurel Real Estate and is asked by Mr. Laurel (Rip Taylor) to make a $400,000 deposit. She absconds with the money and comes up missing. Her sister Lily (Joanna Pacula) seeks out Fostar and together they look for Jane, while Detective Martin Balsam (Martin Balsam) investigates her disappearance to retrieve the money. Jane stops at the Cemetery Motel and checks into room 13, where she meets the innkeeper Antonio Motel (Ezio Greggio ala Norman Bates). The shower scene from *Psycho* is spoofed, and in the end, at the *Psycho* House, all the kooky characters collide to reveal they are all someone else in disguise. In the last shot of the movie, Antonio Motel takes a shower and is stabbed by Alfred Hitchcock (for ruining his movie *Psycho*) who takes off his mask and is revealed to be someone unexpected.

EZIO GREGGIO (Antonio Motel)

When *The Silence of the Hams* debuted in 1984, Ezio was a household name in Europe, as famous as Robin Williams was throughout the world. In Italy, he hosted *Striscia la notizia* or *Strip the News* (1988–2009), a funny look at current news. He made two more American movies as star, producer, and director: *The Good Bad Guy* that also starred Mel Brooks alums Dom DeLuise and Ron Carey and *Screw Loose,* which starred Mel Brooks.

DOM DELUISE (Doctor Animal)

Dom was in the best of Mel Brooks movies: *Blazing Saddles, Silent Movie, History of the World: Part 1, Spaceballs,* and *Robin Hood: Men in Tights.* He and Burt Reynolds teamed up on such hits as *Smokey and the Bandit, The Cannonball Run,* and *The Best Little Whorehouse in Texas.* He also starred in another Ezio Greggio film: *The Good Bad Guy.*

BILLY ZANE (Joe Dee Fostar)

Besides starring in *Titanic* as Cal Hockley, Billy's first big break came as the antagonist in the Australian movie *Dead Calm* opposite a young Nicole Kidman. From playing himself in *Zoolander 2* to starring in *The Phantom* and *Tombstone,* Billy has been in over 100 films and television projects.

JOANNA PACULA (Lily)
Gaining fame for her performance in *Gorky Park* opposite William Hurt, Joanna also starred in *Tombstone* with Kurt Russell, *Virus* with Jamie Leigh Curtis and William Baldwin, and *Forget About It* with Burt Reynolds and Raquel Welch.

CHARLENE TILTON (Jane)
Besides starring as Lucy Ewing on *Dallas*, and on the *Dallas* reboot from 2002-2004, Charlene has been in other comedies like *Problem Child 2* with John Ritter and *Dickie Roberts: Former Child Star* opposite David Spade. She has been in countless film and TV shows.

Martin Balsam (Detective Martin Balsam)
In 1965, Mr. Balsam won an Oscar for Best Actor in a Supporting Role for *A Thousand Clowns*. He was also in *Cape Fear* with Robert DeNiro, *All the Presidents Men* with Robert Redford and Dustin Hoffman, *Murder on the Orient Express* with Ingrid Bergman and Sean Connery, *Breakfast at Tiffany's* with Audrey Hepburn, and played Det. Milton Arbogast in Alfred Hitchcock's *Psycho*.

STUART PANKIN (Inspector Pete Putrid)
Seen in *Fatal Attraction* with Michael Douglas and Glenn Close, Stuart was in *Arachnophobia* with Jeff Daniels for director Frank Marshall, and *Striptease* with Demi Moore. This funnyman has been seen in numerous television shows like *Curb Your Enthusiasm*, *Desperate Housewives*, and *Dharma and Greg*, to name a few. He also voiced the popular puppet character Earl Sinclair in the 1990s Jim Henson sitcom *Dinosaurs*.

JOHN ASTIN (The Ranger)
Besides starring as Gomez Addams in *The Addams Family*, John played Jodie Foster's father in Disney's *Freaky Friday*, was seen in *National Lampoon's European Vacation*, and in season 2 of *Batman* with Adam West, he played The Riddler.

PHYLLIS DILLER (Mr. Laurel's Secretary)
Ms. Diller's had a long lasting friendship with Bob Hope, and was seen in several of his television specials and co-starred in three of his broad 1960s comedy films: *Boy, Did I Get a Wrong Number!*, *Eight on the Lam* and *The Private Navy of Sgt. O'Farrell*. An American Comedic Icon, Diller was seen on scores of television shows including *Laugh-In*, *The Dean Martin Show* and *Hollywood Squares*. She voiced Disney/Pixar's *A Bugs Life* as the Queen, and was seen with Burt Reynolds and Raquel Welch in *Forget About It*!

Larry Storch (Sergeant)

A television Icon, Mr. Storch starred as Corporal Randolph Agarn in the popular TV series *F-Troop* from 1965-67. He guested on countless TV shows like *The Sonny and Cher Comedy Hour, Fantasy Island, The Love Boat, The Hardy Boys/Nancy Drew Mysteries,* and *Mannix*. He was also seen in *The Great Race* with Jack Lemmon and Tony Curtis and *Airport* with Charlton Heston.

RIP TAYLOR (Mr. Laurel)

Forever known as "The King of Camp and Confetti," Rip Taylor got his big break on *The Ed Sullivan Show* in 1964. As a serious actor he was Demi Moore's boss in *Indecent Proposal* and Kate Hudson's father in *Alex & Emma*, directed by Rob Reiner. Other notable campy performances can be seen in Chuck Barris' *The Gong Show Movie; Repossessed* (*The Exorcist* spoof), with Linda Blair and Leslie Nielsen. He also voiced many cartoon characters.

SHELLEY WINTERS (Mrs. Motel/The Mother)

Receiving her first Oscar nomination in *A Place in the Sun* (1951) opposite Elizabeth Taylor and Montgomery Clift, Ms. Winters went on to win two Oscars for her performances in *A Patch of Blue* (1965) and for *The Diary of Anne Frank* (1959). She also won a Golden Globe for *The Poseidon Adventure* (1972). She guested on *Roseanne* as Nana Mary for 10 episodes.

NEDRA VOLZ (Ranger's Wife)

At age 65, Ms. Volz made her film debut in *Your Three Minutes Are Up* starring Beau Bridges. She delighted audiences in television sitcoms for two decades in shows like *Filthy Rich*, *The Dukes of Hazzard*, *Diff'rent Strokes*, and *Mary Hartman, Mary Hartman*. She can be seen in other film comedies such as *Mortuary Academy* and *Earth Girls are Easy*.

Andre Rosey Brown (Motorcycle Cop)

Known for his roles in *Throw Momma from the Train* with Billy Crystal, *Tango & Cash* with Kurt Russell, *Space Jam* with Michael Jordan, and *Kingpin* with Woody Harrelson, Mr. Brown was also seen in many popular television shows such as *The Drew Carey Show*, *The Jamie Foxx Show*, and *MADtv*.

HENRY SILVA (Police Chief)

In *Ocean's Eleven* with the original Rat Pack, Mr. Silva also starred with Frank Sinatra in two other films: *The Manchurian Candidate* and *Contract on Cherry Street*. He can also be seen with Burt Reynolds in *Sharky's Machine* and *Cannonball Run II*. On television he played Buck Rogers' evil adversary in *Buck Rogers in the 25th Century*.

MARSHALL BELL (Cross-Dressing Agent)
Best known for playing George/Kuato in Schwarzenegger's version of *Total Recall*, Marshall was also in *Twins* with Arnold, and can be seen in other notable films such as *Operation Jumbo Drop* with Danny Glover, *Dick Tracy* with Warren Beatty, and *Tucker: The Man and His Dream* with Jeff Bridges.

JOHN ROARKE (Ex-President George Bush)
Not only did John play George Bush in *Hams*, but played him again in *The Naked Gun 2½: The Smell of Fear* with Leslie Nielson, and in *Courage Under Fire* with Denzel Washington. He can be seen in old television classics like *Colombo, Charles in Charge,* and *The Fresh Prince of Bel-Air.*

PAT RICK (President Bill Clinton)
Pat has been impersonating Bill Clinton for most of career and was also seen on *The Daily Show* with Jon Stewart.

TONY COX (Guard)
Tony played Marcus Skidmore in *Bad Santa* and *Bad Santa 2* opposite Billy Bob Thornton. He was also in *Oz the Great and Powerful* with James Franco, *Epic Movie* with Kal Penn, and *Disaster Movie* with Carmen Electra.

JOE DANTE (Dying Man)
Joe Dante directed *Gremlins* and *Gremlins 2: The New Batch*, as well as *The Burbs* starring Tom Hanks. Some episodic television credits include *Steven Spielberg's Amazing Stories* (*The Greibble* starring Haley Mills), *The Twilight Zone*, *Police Squad* and 10 episodes of the reboot of *Hawaii Five-O*.

JOHN CARPENTER (Trenchcoat Man/Gimp)
John Carpenter has directed classic horror films like *Halloween*, *The Fog*, and *The Thing*, and noted sci-fi stories like *Escape from New York* with Kurt Russell and *Starman* starring Jeff Bridges.

JOHN LANDIS (FBI Agent)
Director of such blockbusters as *Animal House* with John Belushi, *An American Werewolf* in London starring David Naughton, *Trading Places* with Dan Aykroyd, *Michael Jackson: Thriller*, *¡Three Amigos!*, and *Coming to America* starring Eddie Murphy.

IRWIN KEYES (Guard)
Character actor Irwin Keyes has been in many notable film such as *The Flintstones* starring John Goodman and Elizabeth Taylor, *Intolerable Cruelty* with George Clooney, and *The Godson* starring Dom DeLuise and Rodney Dangerfield.

KIMBER SCISSONS (Push-Up Lady)
Starring opposite Chip Mayer in *Innocent Adultery*, Kimber was also a series regular on *Sea Hunt* with Ron Ely, and appeared on other notable shows like *Dallas*, *China Beach*, and *Melrose Place*. She has recently appeared several times on the *Housewives of Beverly Hills* as Camille Grammer's friend.

EDDIE DEEZAN (Video Cameraman)
Playing Eugene in *Grease* and *Grease 2*, Eddie's infectious personality and talent has landed him in other films such as *I Wanna Hold Your Hand* with Nancy Allen, and *Mob Boss* with Morgan Fairchild. He lends his unique voice to cartoons such as *SpongeBob SquarePants*, *Pound Puppies*, and *Transformers: Robots in Disguise*.

KEN DAVITAN (Luciano Pavarotti)
Ken Davitan shot to fame starring with Sasha Baron Cohen in *Borat: Cultural Learnings of America for Make Benefit Glorious Nation of Kazakhstan,* playing Azamat. He was also in *S.W.A.T.* with Samuel L. Jackson, *Get Smart* with Steve Carrell, and played Xerxes in *Meet the Spartans*.

PETER DELUISE (Checkout Guard)
Rising to fame in *21 Jump Street* with Johnny Depp, Peter went on to star in *Seaquest DSV* alongside Roy Scheider. He went on to direct several episodes of *Andromeda*, *Stargate SG-1* and *Stargate: Atlantis*.

RUDY DELUCA (Malicious Mel, The Checkout Maniac)

Rudy has had some memorable moments in Mel Brooks movies such as the killer in *High Anxiety*, Captain Mucas in *History of the World: Part I*, and Vinnie in *Spaceballs*. He wrote and directed *Transylvania 6-5000* with Jeff Goldblum, and also was credited as writer on these Mel Brooks films *Silent Movie, High Anxiety, Life Stinks, Dracula: Dead and Loving It,* and *Screw Loose*.

DAVID DELUISE (Policeman #1)

David starred in *Wizards of Waverly Place* as Jerry Russo, playing Selena Gomez's father. He's also been seen in *Golden Shoes* with John Rhys-Davies, and plays Steven in the *Pup Star* franchise. He can currently be seen playing Dean Romano on the television series *The Adventures of Velvet Prozak*.

AL RUSCIO (Phillip Morris)

Mr. Ruscio played Tony Genero in *Al Capone* starring Rod Steiger in 1959. He can also be seen in *Any Which Way You Can* starring Clint Eastwood, *Romero* with Raul Julia, *Showgirls* with Kyle MacLachlin, and *The Phantom* starring Billy Zane and Catherine Zeta-Jones.

DOM IRRERA (Gas Station Attendant)
Stand-Up comedian Dom Irrera has been seen in such films as *The Big Lebowski* with Jeff Bridges, *The 4th Tenor* with Rodney Dangerfield, and *The Bronx Bull* with Joe Mantegna.

LANCE KINSEY (Interrogating Officer)
Mr. Kinsey played Sergeant/Captain Proctor in the *Police Academy* franchise. He was also in *Loaded Weapon* with Emilio Estevez, and in *BuzzKill* with Krysten Ritter.

DANIEL MCVICAR (Forensics Expert)
Daniel played Clarke Garrison on *The Bold and the Beautiful* from 1987–2009. He can also be seen in *Screw Loose* with Ezio Greggio and Mel Brooks. Currently he can be seen in *Creators: The Past* with William Shatner.

MATTEO MOLINARI (Bellboy)

Matteo won the role of the Bellboy, the only actor in a scene with Mel Brooks in *Hams*. He can also be seen in *The Good Bad Guy* with Ezio Greggio.

MEL BROOKS (Checkout Guest)

Classic Mel Brooks movies include *Blazing Saddles, High Anxiety, Young Frankenstein, History of the World: Part I, Silent Movie, Robin Hood: Men in Tights, Dracula: Dead and Loving It, The Producers*, and *Spaceballs*.

WILHELM VON HOMBURG (Maître D')

Wilhelm played Vigo in *Ghostbusters II*, and can also be seen in *Die Hard* with Bruce Willis, *In the Mouth of Madness* with Sam Neill, and *The Package* with Gene Hackman.

LANA SCHWAB (Nurse)
Lana was in Clint Eastwood's *The Bridges of Madison County,* and also starred with Ned Beatty in *The Exorcist* spoof movie *Repossessed.*

LONNIE BURR (Drunk)
An original Mouseketeer with Annette Funicello, Lonnie went on to appear in nearly forty movies and television shows. Some notable television shows are *The New Gidget* and *Chicago Hope.*

HEATHER-ELIZABETH PARKHURST (Beautiful Woman)
Heather can be seen in *Beverly Hills Cop III* with Eddie Murphy and *Body of Evidence* with Nick Cassavetes and Sandahl Bergman. She can be seen on such TV shows as *NYPD Blue, Wings* and *Pacific Blue.*

Pre-Production

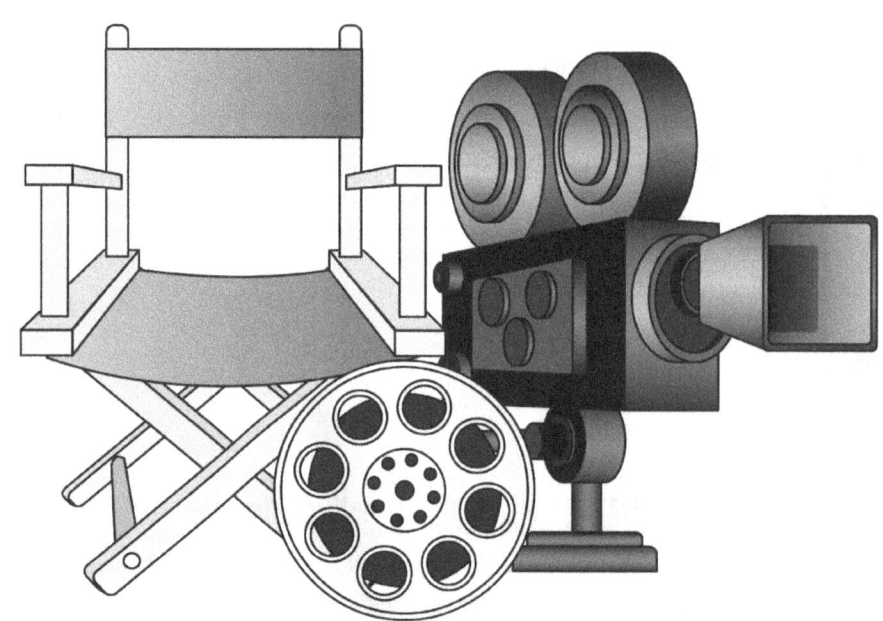

Ezio Greggio, our Star, Writer, Producer, and Director, with Julie Corman, our Producer, whose husband is Roger Corman, a trailblazer in the world of independent film.

Meeting Billy Zane for the first time in the production office. He came with a hamlet haircut and instantly started telling jokes and making me laugh. "To be a ham, or not to be ham. That is the bacon."

Alexis Cahill, our First Assistant Director, was on a deadline to finish the schedule working long hours. I swung by to cheer him up! It worked!

Production Designer James Newport on the right and his assistant.

Producer Julie Corman, Isabel Henderson (post production supervisor), and Whitney Hunter (Unit Production Manager). I wonder if they are dreaming of ham sandwiches for lunch.

Phyllis Diller and Casting Director Craig Campobasso (Yep! That's me.) This is the day when Ms. Diller came into the office to meet Ezio Greggio and show him all her VHS performances, since he (living in Italy) did not know who she was. Phyllis was a great sport. She told me, "I'll take the part even without reading the script just because of the name of the film," and then let loose one of her famous cackles.

Casting Memories

Charlene Tilton came in to meet Ezio to discuss a cameo role and got the lead of Jane.

(Right) Andre Rosey Brown hamming it up with Ezio during his first meeting to play a gay cop.

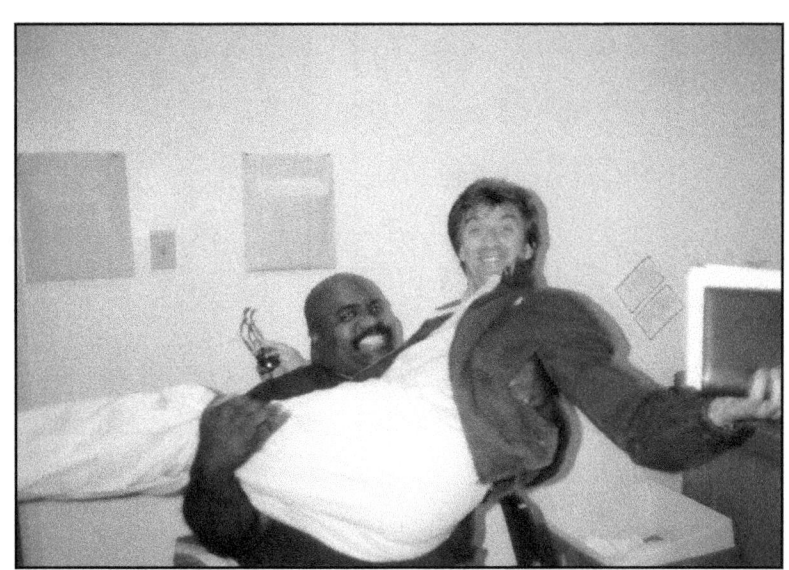

Nedra Volz on her audition day with me. She was so funny and told the dirtiest clean jokes.

Below are more mugs who got parts.

Lonnie Burr
Drunk

Rip Taylor
Mr. Laurel

Wilhelm von Homburg
Maitre D

The Silence of the Hams: A Pictorial Memoir

(Right) John Roarke
Ex-President George Bush Sr.

(Right) Shelly Desai
Trick

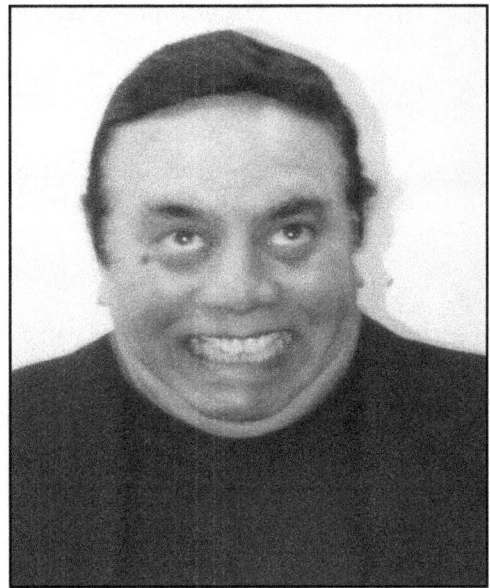

(Left) Dom Irrera
Gas Station Attendant

Two-time Emmy award-winning actress Eileen Davidson, who starred as Ashley on *The Young and the Restless,* and on *Days of Our Lives* as the deliciously evil Kristen DiMera, was also a *Beverly Hills Housewife* for three years. She auditioned for the part of Lily.

I brought Zelda Rubinstein (*Poltergeist* movies) in the meet Ezio to see if we could squeeze her into a role. But most of the parts were taken by this time. What a talent this lady was. She passed away in 2010.

Rob Pilatus was a member of the pop music duo Milli Vanilli, alongside Fabrice Morvan. We could not find anything suitable to him. He passed away in 1998.

Kimberlin Brown at the time was very popular playing crazy Sheila on *Young and the Restless* and *Bold and the Beautiful*. We did offer her a role as a model, one of the only parts left, but due to her soap schedule, we could not make it work.

Popular character actress Dody Goodman, whom starred in both *Grease* movies, also starred in *Private Resort* with Johnny Depp. Wish we could have found something for this talented lady. She passed away in 2008.

Jack Harrell was a regular performer and announcer for *The Sonny and Cher Show.*

Prior to *Hams,* Jack introduced me to Lisa Hartman, and I worked as her assistant on *The Lisa Hartman Special* in 1976. Everyone thought I was Lisa's brother. He passed away in 1999.

Louis Lombardi, at the beginning of his illustrious career, came in for a role. Although we did not hire him, he went on to be in over seventy movies and television shows, including *The Usual Suspects* with Benicio Del Toro, and *Natural Born Killers* with Woody Harrelson.

The Production

We began principal photography on April 12, 1993, in Griffith Park, Los Angeles proper, near the Merry-Go-Round. The first day we shot the training course scene with Jo Dee Fostar (Billy Zane), Ex-President Bush (John Roarke), and then-President Bill Clinton (Pat Rick). The next scene up was Billy Zane doing push-ups on top of Kimber Sissons. The last scenes of the day were the establishing shots of the Hollywood Nuthouse. On May 27, the last shooting day, we filmed Larry Storch (Sergeant) and Billy Zane doing their first gag together in the film.

Those FBI guys get the best workout equipment.

The Silence of the Hams cast. Director Ezio Greggio (seated) and me—casting director Craig Campobasso (kneeling) amid cast members (from left) Stuart Pankin, Billy Zane, Martin Balsam, Henry Silva, Rip Taylor, Charlene Tilton, Dom DeLuise, Bubba Smith, Rosey Brown, Shelley Winters, Jeff Bright (the Mummy) and John Astin.

The Silence of the Hams: A Pictorial Memoir

Here I am hamming it up with stars Dom DeLuise (Doctor Animal) and Ezio Greggio (Antonio Motel). Ezio was also the star, writer and director and everything he said on the list tacked outside his trailer. He enjoyed being called the "Grande Formaggio." That's Italian for Big Cheese.

Celebrating Ezio's birthday on April 7, 1993. Julie Corman (Producer) got him this great cake and the gift in his hand. I wonder what she got him?

(Bottom) The crew celebrating Ezio's birthday on our soundstage behind the unfinished *Psycho* house interior. Julie gave him a leather bound script of T*he Silence of the Hams!*

(Top) The bumbling Sargent (Larry Storch) is always in physical peril. Jo Dee Fostar (Billy Zane) trips him up—literally! This was shot on our last day of shooting.

(Bottom) Directors John Carpenter (Trenchcoat Man/Gimp) and Joe Dante (dying man). They had fun as actors for the day spoofing their favorite genre.

(Top) Even the opening sequence of the film spoofed the MGM lion. Here the wolf howls and then coughs. As one reviewer put it, "If this makes you laugh then he didn't have to say something else." And laugh we did.

Films are not always shot in sequence. There are a lot of factors like location, lighting and who is going to be on set on a particular day.

(Left) Ezio Greggio (Antonio Motel) gets stabbed by a mysterious person in the opening sequence of the film. This sets everything in motion. We, the audience, won't find out who the murderer is until the big reveal at the end and not until the very last frame.

(Right) That's me with the extinguished and beloved actor Henry Silva who played the Police Chief. Henry was so excited to come and play with us. He's in the opening sequence with Eddie Deezan, and directors John Carpenter and Joe Dante.

(Left) One of the iconic horror films spoofed in this film is *Psycho*. Here is James R. Einolf, our sound mixer, who got into the spirit of the film, having his very own MRS. BATES director's chair.

(Top Right) Ezio told Martin Balsam he would win another Academy Award for his performance in *Hams*. Martin laughed. So did Ezio.

(Lower Right) Me, Kimber Scissons and Billy Zane.

The Silence of the Hams: A Pictorial Memoir

(Top) First day and first shot of filming. Billy Zane and John Roarke between shots. Pat Rick played then President Bill Clinton, and John Roarke, Ex-President George Bush. Location Griffith Park.

(Bottom Left) Pat Rick getting a Bill Clinton nose.

(Bottom Right) Pat Rick with his finished Clinton nose job and eye concealer.

The Silence of the Hams: A Pictorial Memoir

Antonio Motel's mother stabs Charlene Tilton's Jane in the famous *Psycho* scene in many ridiculous ways. Wait! That's a picture of Ezio Greggio. I thought I cast Shelley Winters in that part. You'll just have to watch the rerelease on Blu-ray to find out.

After Jane steals Mr. Laurel's $400,000 she heads for the Cemetery Motel where there is always a vacancy. She is caught in a torrential downpour. When she can no longer see out the window, the camera pulls back, and Jane gives the crew guys hosing the car a look. They apologize, "Sorry, Charlene. My bad."

The Silence of the Hams: A Pictorial Memoir

Jane's conscience gets to her as she amscrays with the stolen money. Jo says, "Won't you take me to funkytown?"

When Jane goes missing, Jo and Lily look for her. But what are they looking at here? Oh, crap. I'm going to have to watch the movie for the umpteenth time to find out.

As Jane showers the haunting *Psycho* music theme plays. She rips open the shower curtain to find a string quintet. She tells them to take five.

Antonio Motel dressed as his Mother kills Jane with countless weapons. Thank goodness he is a lousy shot.

The Silence of the Hams: A Pictorial Memoir

(Left) Ezio Greggio with his director's hat on setting up a shot, with DP Jacques Haitkin (in middle) in downtown Los Angeles.

(Right) Rudy DeLuca plays Malicious Mel, the Checkout Maniac, the name Ezio gave him as an homage to Mel Brooks, whom Rudy has written many movies for.
(Bottom Left) Peter in the make-up chair getting ready for his scene.
(Bottom Right) Rudy and Peter DeLuise, the checkout guard, rehearse their scene.

(Left) Larry Storch, Me and Ezio Greggio taking a picture for the mutual admiration club!

(Left) Irwin Keyes, the guard at the Hollywood Nuthouse takes Jo Dee Fostar (Zane) into the Unbelievably Bad Maniacs Wing where Jo meets Doctor Animal.

I also cast Irwin in another spoof movie *The Godson* starring Rodney Dangerfield and Dom DeLuise who both played Godfathers. He was one of the best character actors around and a great guy.

The Silence of the Hams: A Pictorial Memoir

Lance Kinsey (*Police Academy* Franchise) was the Interrogating Officer. He questioned Sharon Bone (Cornelia Johnsson) in a spoof segment of *Basic Instinct*.

Wait till you see what happens when she uncrosses her legs.

Jo drives up the hill to the Hollywood Nuthouse. I hope he likes mixed nuts.

Jo can't drive for sh@#. But he looks good. That's all that matters. Eat your heart out James Bond.

The Silence of the Hams: A Pictorial Memoir

(Top) Jo Dee Fostar had to show his ID to get into the Hollywood Nuthouse. Billy improvised and grabbed a waffle from the craft service table.

(Bottom) When the camera reverses Irwin Keyes is holding up this plank to make it appear as the large door to the Hollywood Nuthouse.

(Top left) With Tony Cox who plays a guard at the Hollywood Nuthouse, and our costume supervisor Allyson Brown (now Allyson B. Fanger). Currently she's the costume designer for *Grace and Frankie*.

(Top Right) Tony Cox on set. From a prison guard in *Hams* to *Bad Santa* with Billy Bob Thornton. Photo courtesy Matteo Molinari.

(Bottom Right) The guard takes Jo to the bad maniacs wing to meet Dr. Animal.

My first appearance in *The Silence of the Hams* with my faux-wife and real life mother Marie Donna King-Campobasso.

I get asked all the time what a casting director does. Here's my CliffsNote definition. I manage the casting of all speaking actors in a film or TV show. I work directly with the director and producer to know what is in the budget for each actor, star and day player alike. I suggest names for each lead role that they can afford, as well as holding auditions. When the producer and director have made their choices, I negotiate the actor deals. On *Hams* I negotiated every deal. On giant studio movies they have lawyers that negotiate star name talent. Another integral part of being a CD is having extensive knowledge of actors and their abilities that fit certain roles. It's likened to being an empath that can look into the soul of the actor and know if you pull the performance out of them or not.

(TopLeft) Momma Marie with Wilhelm von Homburg (Vigo the Carpathian in *Ghostbusters II*) played the Maître D' in the scene where Billy Zane, at the Hollywood Nuthouse, goes through unexpected and ridiculous places before he meets with Doctor Animal.

(Right) Wilhelm tried choking me into giving him a bigger part.

(Top Left) Billy helping me out of that disgusting moat.

(Bottom left) In my second appearance in the film, right after the previous restaurant scene, I am an aggressive shark lawyer in the water pit. We wore fishing waders with our jackets over it.

(Bottom Right) Ezio grabbed a fun photo opportunity. I kept the DANGER! LAWYERS sign as a souvenir from the movie.

Dr. Animal flies into frame spoofing Gary Oldman's *Dracula*.

Dr. Animal was also a bad psychic. He thought Jo was a black woman from Cleveland.

"Of all the things I miss, I think I miss my mind the most!" –Dr. Animal

The Silence of the Hams: A Pictorial Memoir

Dom DeLuise made everyone laugh on set, especially with his improvisations. It was hard not to laugh during every take. My favorite moment is when he asks Jo, "Was the ham silent? Ham can be very quiet unless it falls down stairs and then it goes boom-de-dee-boom-boom-boom."

Dr. Animal was just about to make his happy noise, "Iggy Boo!" I still can't figure out how he goes to the bathroom in that toilet.

Iggy Boo!

The Silence of the Hams: A Pictorial Memoir

Gomez Addams and Dr. Animal. A glass of Chianti followed.

I got to work with Dom many times. I could hardly wait to get to set every day. He was one of the true comedic greats and one amazing human being.

(Top) Shelley, Dom and Rip. Three geniuses.

(Bottom) Ezio putting on his directorial hat. He was telling Billy and Dom how to make al dente pasta.

The Silence of the Hams: A Pictorial Memoir

Pavarotti (Ken Davitan) sang and Billy Zane, Stuart Pankin and Daniel McVicar were mesmerized. Then Pavarotti had an accident. You'll have to watch the movie to find out what happened.

Happy bright shining faces were the modus operandi on the set every day. Dom, Billy, John and me. Can you tell I loved this job!

We shot *Hams* on 35 millimeter film. Our Editors Robert Barrere and Andy Horvitch cut the film using their skills and technique to move from scene-to-scene, pushing the action forward to hold the audience captive. One of the first films made in 1898, *Come Along, Do!* featured more than one shot. To establish continuity, British filmmaker Robert W. Paul's film editing established continuity, involving action that sewed sequences together.

(Top Left) In Mr. Laurel's Real Estate Office. Me, Bubba Smith, Charlene Tilton, Ezio Greggio and Phyllis Diller. Bubba is standing on 10 apple boxes.

(Bottom Left) Before she got into black-eye make-up, Phyllis Diller showed off her *Hams* T-Shirt!

(Bottom Right) Phyllis Diller's secretary has a few accidents and gets a black eye. We all had fun taking pictures, pretending to sock-it-to-her! She got a kick out of that.

(Top Left) Our pint-sized actresses Charlene and Nedra.

(Bottom Left) Charlene Tilton, Rip Taylor and Charlene's double get goofy. The set was a license to be your most authentic silly self!

(Bottom Right) My favorite picture of Charlene and I on set. What fun we had!

The Silence of the Hams: A Pictorial Memoir

Looking good Charlene. Marilyn Monroe would be proud.

Outside Phyllis Diller's trailer with her stunt woman. No comediennes were hurt in the making of this movie.

See what happens when you don't learn your lines.

(Top) Charlene getting ready to shoot the scene after she steals Mr. Laurel's $400,000 dollars. This scene was shot on Roscoe Blvd. in Panorama City.

(Right) The crew getting everything ready for the scene with Charlene in the getaway car after she steals the money. Base camp was at the Panorama Bowl.

The Silence of the Hams: A Pictorial Memoir

(Top Right) Charlene's character Jane sleeps in her car the night she steals Mr. Laurel's money. She wakes up to Rosey Brown's gay cop wrapping on her window. He asks her for her driver's license. When she gets out her large wallet, a giant condom falls out. She says, "That's my boyfriend Jo's." Rosey replies in a soft voice, "Can I have Jo's phone number."

(Top Left) Joanna Pacula and Billy Zane prepping for the scene where Lily visits her sister's boyfriend Jo to tell him she's missing. Photo Courtesy: Matteo Molinari.

(Bottom Right) Rosey Brown was a cop in real life. He asked me when he got the part how he should study to play a gay cop. I told him to go to a gay bar and observe. He went to West Hollywood, spent a few hours there, and then called me laughing, "Craig, I got 3 phone numbers." Then continued laughing, saying that when he left the bar, a cop car pulled over, and his colleagues said, "Rosey, what in the world are you doing at a gay bar?" He explained it was for a part. The guys at the station (and his wife) ragged him for the longest time. He was such a good sport. Just loved this man.

Rosey holding Jo's condom.

Director Ezio Greggio directing Al Ruscio (Phillip Morris) and famed director John Landis (FBI agent).

(Right) Detective Martin Balsam checks out all the hotels in the areas to find Jane. He drives by *The Exorcist* Motel and the mannequin heads spins. That's First AD Alexis Cahill in the far back and Joe Rice extras coordinator in jacket.

The Silence of the Hams: A Pictorial Memoir

(Top Left) That's me standing outside Jack The Ripper Motor Inn where Mel Brooks' cameo took place.

(Top Right) Mel tips Matteo Molinari, the Bell Boy a quarter and says, "Have a party." Matteo is also one of our beloved crew members. He was the videographer for the behind-the-scenes footage.

(Right) The best expressions are left to the imagination.

(Top) The Ranger attempts to scare Jo and Lily at the bowling alley. (Bottom Left) Jo shaves, takes a towel to dab his face, then when he sets the towel on the counter he has a full beard. (Bottom Right) Martin Balsam and I have a few laughs before going to the set.

(Top) From Left to right: David DeLuise, Ezio Greggio, Dom DeLuise and Billy Zane. Ezio is rehearsing them outside of Doctor Animal's Pizza Place which use to be Famous Amos cookies on Sunset Blvd.

(Bottom left) I'm standing outside the Ranger's House (John Astin) that we used for the interior. The exterior was a tiny old house in the slums.

(Bottom right) Playing an extra, my Mom Marie hammed it up for the camera. Now you know where I get it from.

(Top) Billy Zane and John Astin rehearsing their interpretive dance sequence.

(Bottom Right) A gag from *The Addams Family*, "Thing's" box contained a foot instead of a hand and lit John Astin's cigar. John says, "Thank you, smelly thing." I had someone use their hand for the photo opportunity.

(Top Left) John and Joanna going over their lines.

The Silence of the Hams: A Pictorial Memoir

Nedra Volz (the Ranger's wife) was so loved by all of us. She was one of the funniest character actresses around. Yes, we coddled her! Who could resist?

(Top) Director of Photgraphy Jacques Haitkin, alongside Producer Julie Corman and First AD Alexis Cahill, set up the shot at the Gas Station where Jo and Lily stop for fuel. Location near Lake Piru, California.

(Bottom) Stand-Up comedian Dom Irrera played the gas station attendant who spy's Lily beauty (Joanna Pacula) and uses the hose as an extension of his sexual desire, as if looking at a Playboy centerfold.

(Top Right) After the gas station attendant has his way with his hose, Lily steps out of the car and is miraculously pregnant. The costume department inserted a basketball under Joanna's dress for the gag.

(Top Left) The sign above Dom Irrera, the gas station attendant takes on a whole new meaning when you know the gag. Note: the sign was a part of the gas station, not put up by our art department.

(Bottom Right) Costumes had two dresses made and had to alter one to fit the basketball.

(Top Left) Me and Alexis Cahill, our First AD. It wasn't hard to make people smile during the shoot. I think everyone's face hurt at the end of the day from the cement grins on all our faces.

(Right) Me standing outside the *Psycho* House with a sign letting everyone know that it's the killer's abode.

(Bottom) The recreation of the Bates Motel (Cemetery Motel in our film) in Santa Clarita, CA. The land was riddled with snakes. They had to have a snake wrangler come and remove them before we shot. I didn't know there were snakes until halfway through the day and I had been wearing shorts. For the rest of the day I kept looking at the ground.

(Top Left) Looked like Bubba Smith lent Nedra his jacket. Wardrobe has been looking for it for 25 years!

(Top Right) Oops! Caught Ezio on the toilet.

(Bottom Right) This was our fake cemetery. Later that night we shot a parody of Michael Jackson's *Thriller*.

The Big Reveal

(Top) Mr. Laurel, Jane and Detective Martin Balsam watch the Cop's reveal played by Rosey Brown.

(Bottom) The Cop is really John Astin, the Ranger.

(Top) The Ranger reveals another secret to Shelley Winters, Antonio Motel's mother.

(Bottom) Greed over the $400,000 ensues. All the characters collide and start taking bets on who everyone's reveal will be.

(Left) The big reveal at the end of the movie where everyone was someone else the whole time. It reminds me of Mary Frann playing Bob Newhart's wife on *Newhart,* which ran from 1982-1990, and on the final episode Suzanne Pleshette wakes up next to Bob in their old bedroom from *The Bob Newhart Show.* Bob says, "Honey, wake up, you won't believe the dream I just had." Or on a *Dallas* season end cliffhanger, Bobby Ewing in the shower, even though he's dead, his wife Pam (Victoria Principle) realizing his death was just a dream. *Dallas* alum Charlene Tilton (Lucy Ewing) quips out of the corner of her mouth in *Hams,* "*Dallas* was never like this!"

Pictured: Charlene Tilton's Jane revealed herself to be Nedra Volz's character the Ranger's wife.

(Bottom Left) Joanna Pacula's Lily reveals she is really Detective Martin Balsam. Charlene Tilton and daughter Cherish watch from the wings.

Billy Zane's character Jo reveals that he is the dead corpse of Antonio Motel.

The Silence of the Hams: A Pictorial Memoir

Getting ready to shoot the last scene in the movie! Sitting high up on the camera truck are director Ezio Greggio and DP Jacques Haitkin.

(Bottom) At the end of the movie all the honeyed hams (our cast) come down the stairs to celebrate with cheerleaders and marching bands. That's Joanna Pacula striking her last hambone pose.

(Top Left) Camera's getting ready to roll as the cast comes down the stairs. That's our Bellboy (with Mel Brooks) and videographer Matteo Molinari coming towards camera.

(Bottom) Bubba Smith (Olaf) relaxing during takes on his cop car, the marching band in background ready to play once the scene starts.

(Top) Pat Rick (President Bill Clinton) playing the clarinet and making Charlene Tilton laugh. I'm sure there was a dirty joke right before I took this picture.

(Bottom) Grabbing a quick picture with this funny lady who I could not stop hugging, Nedra Volz.

Getting a quick picture with megastar and two time Academy Award winning actress Shelley Winters. She's wearing our *Silence of the Hams* hat, a gift to cast and crew at the end of production. This is one of many pictures that Shelley and I took and in almost all of them her eyes are closed. Emoji: frustrated face.

(Top) Ezio (Antonio Motel) and Dom DeLuise (Dr. Animal) shooting some publicity shots before the last big scene at the *Psycho* House.

(Bottom Right) Hair and make-up putting the final touches on the actors before the cast picture of comedic greats. Joanna Pacula, Billy Zane, Dom DeLuise, and John Astin.

The Silence of the Hams: A Pictorial Memoir

We finally arrive at the last scene in the movie to find out who stabbed Antonio Motel at the beginning of the movie.

The *Jurassic Pork* poster for a movie that was going to be next for Ezio. Sadly, it was never made.

But wait! There is still one final reveal! Alfred Hitchcock peels off his mask and he's Doctor Animal! Dom was very claustrophobic wearing that mask. It was tight and made him sweat profusely. With the Hitchcock eyes built into the mask he was also walking blindly into the scene. Not wanting to do the scene twice, he nailed it in one take and that's what you see in the movie.

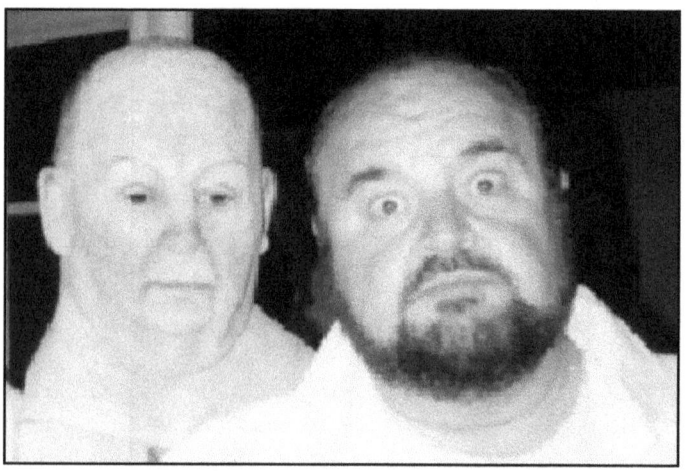

The Silence of the Hams: A Pictorial Memoir

Mel Brooks: The King of Comedy

(Left) Wednesday, May 12, 1993 finally arived with much excitement! It was the day Mel Brooks was coming to shoot his cameo. Ezio had this MEL BROOKS sign with a King's crown made up to hang on the outside of his dressing trailer.

(Bottom) Mel Brooks' Dressing Room. Ezio sitting in the King's chair he had brought in for Mel Brooks and a King's septer, along with candelabra and fruit basket.

All of my childhood dreams came true meeting this comedic icon! Oh, and, he brought his wife, Anne Bancroft to set too! The cast and crew, including me, funnybones were tickled.

The Sets

Film sets are as important to the atmosphere of the story as casting the right actors. Here are some photos of our sets and locations in no particular order of appearance. To the left is the *Psycho* House Parlor. Below are two shots of the *Psycho* House Foyer.

(Above) Balsam recreates his famous fall in Hitchcock's original *Psycho* from 1960; only we have him flying over freeways, in clouds, over people running, etc.

Here are some of the interior sets like Jane's room 13 at the Cemetery Motel. Actually all the rooms were #13. I see a shower in her future.

Another angle of Jane's motel room.

The gondola that swims by Jo's high rise apartment window with tourists.

Dr. Animal's Pizza Place offers fine cannibal cuisine.

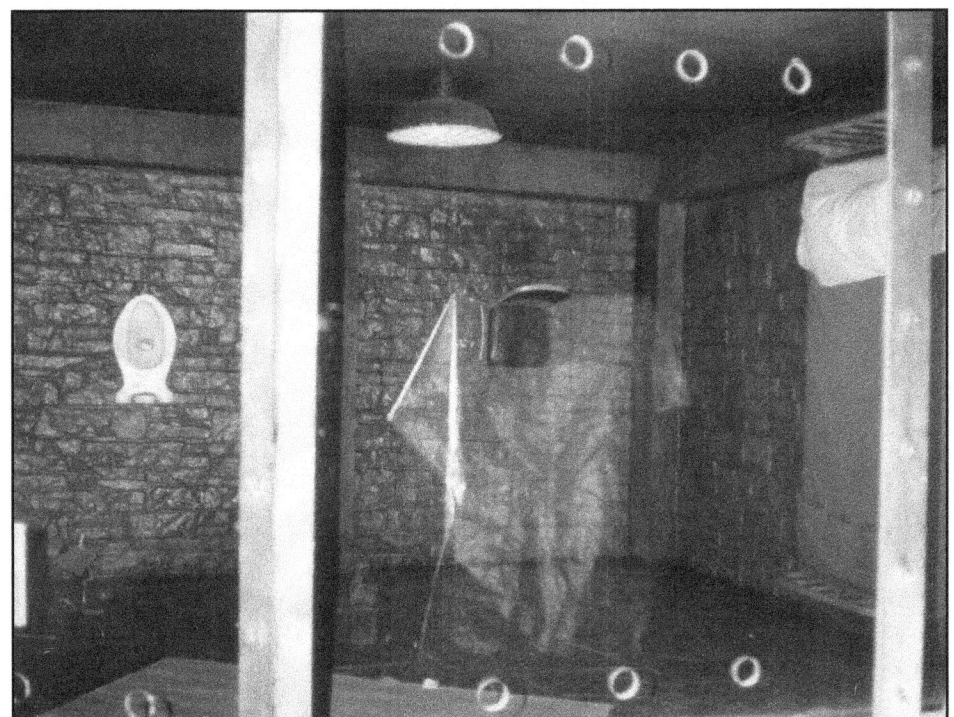

(Left) Dr. Animal's jail cell. Jo Dee Fostar visits him to find out who the killer is.

(Bottom) The bed was attached to the wall and Dr. Animal would jump up and lay on it defying the laws of gravity.

(Bottom Right) Laurel Real Estate Offices. Phyllis Diller, Bubba Smith, and Rip Taylor concentrating before they shoot their scene.

Heather-Elizabeth Parkhurst (who played the beautiful woman) in front of the eye painting from which Antonio Motel looked through from a secret room to spy on Jane.

(Bottom) A peeping Antonio hides behind the many eyes on the other side of the wall. Jane is unaware that he is sharpening his knife in anticipation of MURDER!

Funny Faces and Behind the Scenes Antics

One of the best things about casting a film with such a variety of actors is you become a big crazy family. Our cast had tremendous comedic talent. Get them together, and they feed off one another. Here is a glimpse into some of the fun we had on and off the set. Think movie montage of hilarity.

(Above) Jo thought she was the purdiest li'l thing he ever did see.
(Right) Me and Dom Irrera. Banana jokes welcome.

Ham and Bacon. Billy and Craig.

Rudy and Craig. Two Purdy guys.

The Silence of the Hams: A Pictorial Memoir

Rosey Brown arriving for work on *Hams*!

(Top) Don't tell Charlene but she's missing her two front teeth.

The comedic duo; aka two cheeseballs!

(Top) Dr. Animal squeezing my lemons.

(Bottom) Mr. Laurel after he got his $400,000 back. Boy was he happy!

Time for a shower, funny face.

A spoof movie parodies other film genres, imitating famous scenes as pastiches. Ezio Greggio stitched horror film themes into *Hams*. This genre parody had not been done before. The first parody movie (1905) ever made was a unfettered remake of director Edwin S. Porter's previous film, *The Great Train Robbery* (1903), but this time, the cast is comprised entirely of children.

These little piggies made ham.

Working long hours on a film set can be grueling and exhausting. Even though we all lacked sleep, every day was a new adventure in hilarity. You never knew what was going to come out of the stars mouths on or off the set. The director sets the tone of the production. And our silly leader Ezio kept us in stitches every day. I remember being in one of the first production lunch meetings with him. We looked at each other at the same time and showed each other our chewed food. I realized then this was going to be the most awesome shoot ever.

The Silence of the Hams: A Pictorial Memoir

(Top) Casting director barbells.

(Bottom Left) Bet my arms are bigger than your arms.

(Bottom Right) Shoulder push-ups. Workout now complete. Thanks Bubba and Rosey.

Who farted? I bet it was that okra, jalapenos and a touch of ginger Peter Putrid had for breakfast.

Pete Putrid's Recipe for Prosciutto Chips

Line a baking pan with parchment paper and preheat oven to 400 degrees.
Lay the prosciutto slices in a circle so they don't burn on baking sheet.
In about 10 minutes they will turn golden brown.
Remove from oven and let cool until they crisp.

(Top) Look what I got the President to do.

(Bottom Left) The President of the Matteo Molinari fan Club. Matteo's sorry too.

(Bottom Right) Took an hour to count all their nose hairs. Alfred had the most. A PA was given the task to pluck them. Took 1 hour and delayed shooting.

(Top) Antonio squeezing Jane. I hope she knows he's the killer. (Bottom Left) Set food. Don't hurl Ezio. We need you for the next shot. (Bottom Middle) Could a spoof of *Hamlet* be next? (Bottom Right) No boobies were harmed in the taking of this picture.

The Silence of the Hams: A Pictorial Memoir

Hams in the make-up and hair trailer!

Famous People Who Visited Our Set

Anne Bancroft came with her husband Mel Brooks when he shot his cameo. Anne loved that I was Italian and was quite engaging. Hollywood royalty! On location in downtown Los Angeles.

The Silence of the Hams: A Pictorial Memoir

Leif Garrett, former singer and teenage heartthrob, a friend of Billy's, came by to hang out with us one day.

(Top Right) Then unknown actor Noah Wyle came by to visit Allyson B. Fanger, known then as Allyson Brown, our costume supervisor. He started a little show called *ER* the following year. Shh! I think these two were dating back then. Don't tell anyone.

(Bottom Left) Billy Zane's sister Lisa and *Laugh In*'s Ruth Buzzi stopped by to join the set laughter.

It's a Wrap

the silence of the hams

an ezio greggio film

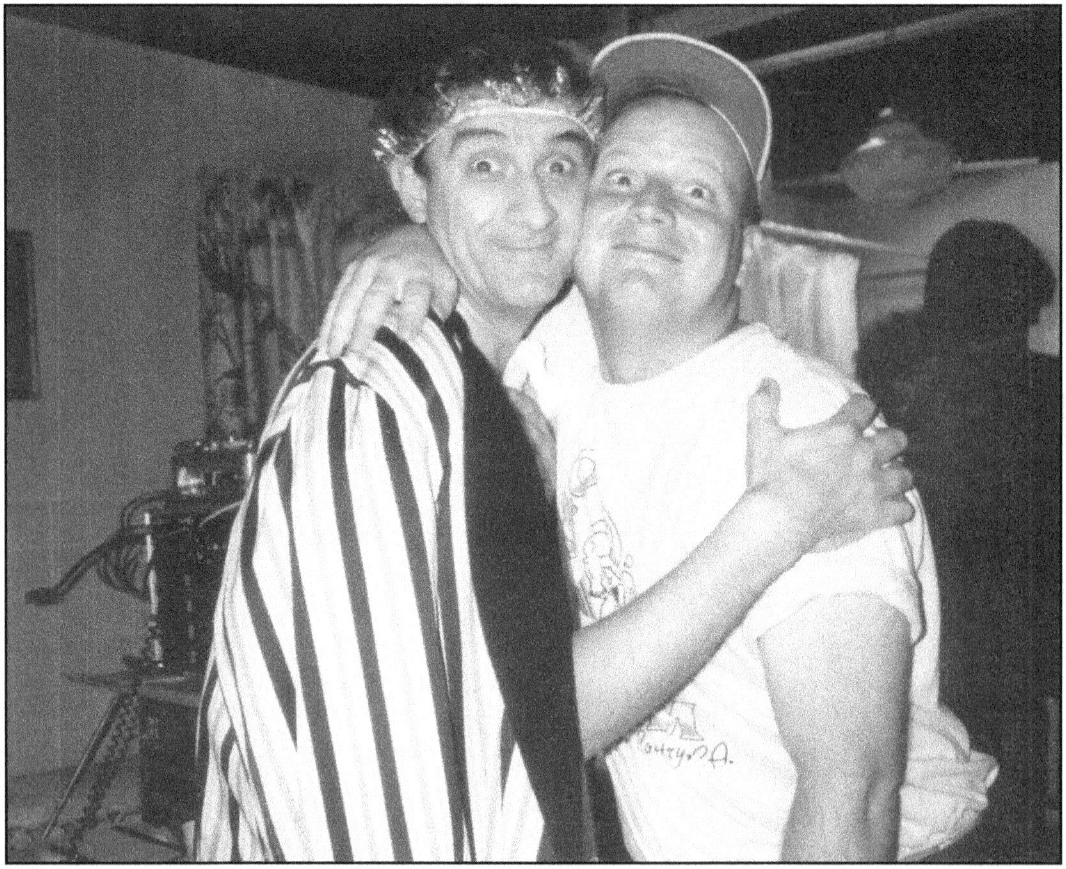

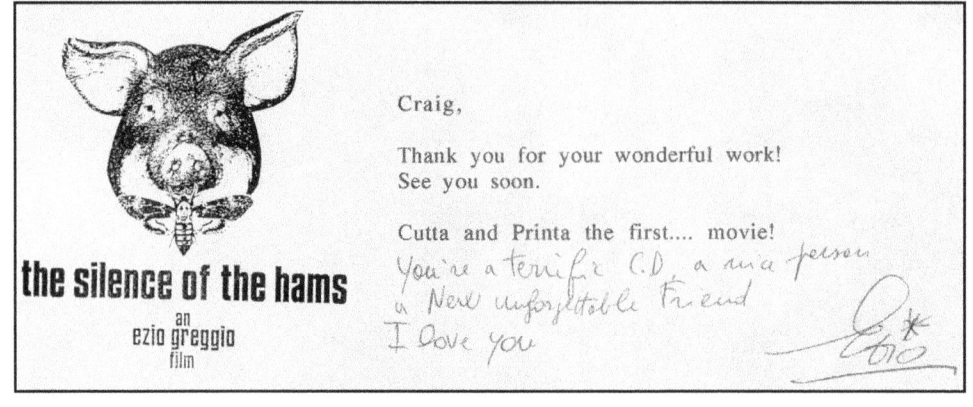

Craig,

Thank you for your wonderful work!
See you soon.

Cutta and Printa the first.... movie!

You're a terrific C.D. a nice person
a New unforgettable Friend
I love you

Ezio

The Silence of the Hams: A Pictorial Memoir

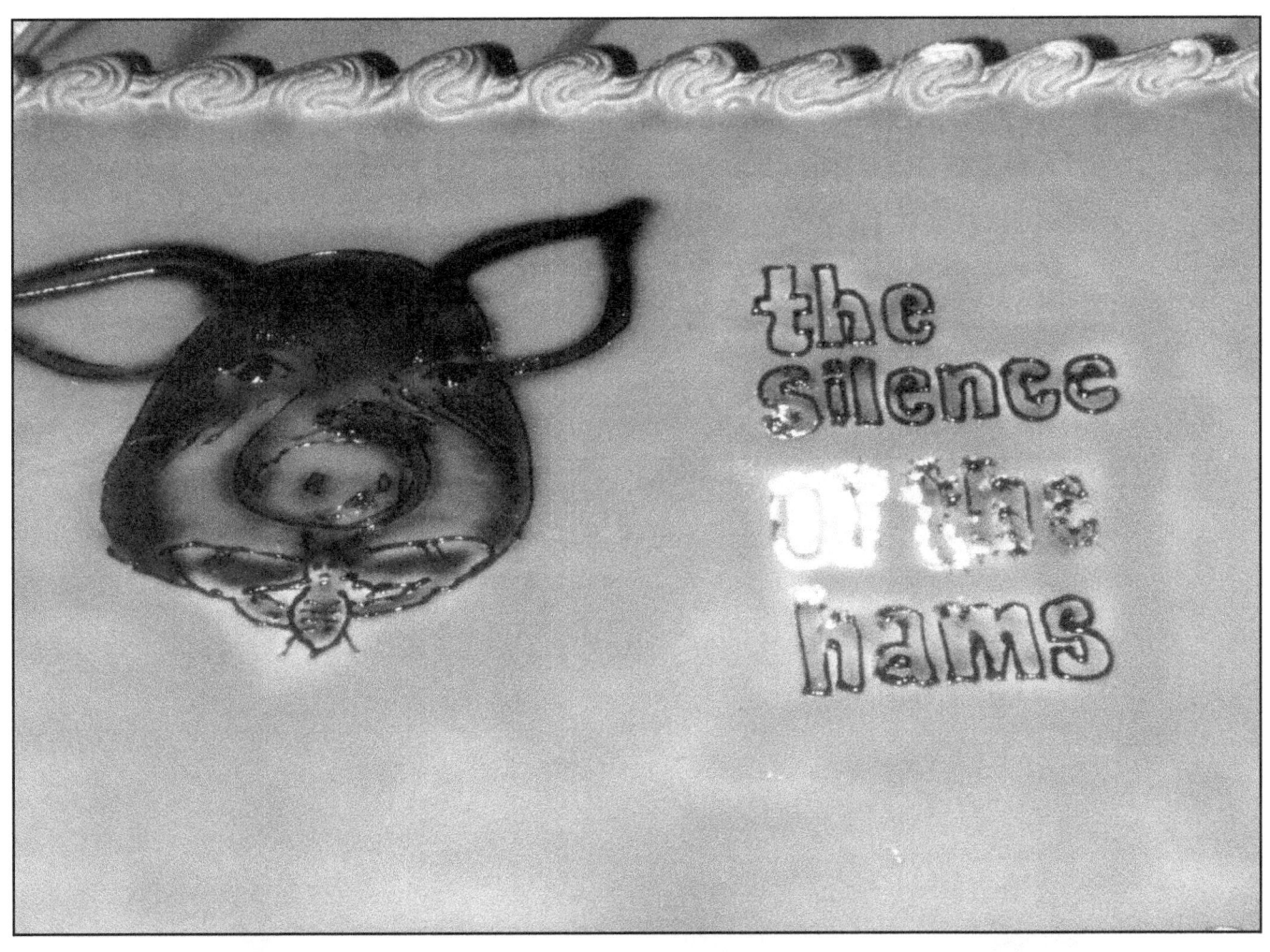

Wrap party cake. Sad looking confection isn't it. The icing was bright red.

MONDAY, MAY 31, 1993
8:00 PM
Ezio invited the cast of The Silence of the Hams to have dinner Italian style.

One of the best things about being together during the filming of a movie is the down time spent having meals to get to know each other better. Of course, it is even better if your director is Italian. Mangia!

(Opposite Page) Shelley Winters, Ezio, and his then wife Isabel.

(Top) Stuart Pankin, Rip Taylor, Matteo Molinari, Charlene Tilton, and Rudy DeLuca recreating the famous Sophia Loren photo looking at Jayne Mansfield's breasts.

San Remo Restaurant

Henry Silva, Charlene Tilton and me.

Marshall Bell and me, whom I worked with on the original *Total Recall*. I called him and asked him to play the cross-dressing cop. He laughed at the concept and said yes immediately.

(Top) Every picture I took with Shelley her eyes were closed. Well, at least her eyes are open here. Now to find the lens.

There's that Ezio funny face. With Johanna Stein, Isabel Greggio and me.

(Right) Joanna Pacula and John Astin. Joanna's hand is covering up pasta sauce spilled on John's suit. He should have worn a cloth napkin bib like the old Italians.

(Top Left) Joanna, me, Charlene and George Christy of "The Hollywood Reporter." George gave the film a wonderful write up in his column.

(Top Right) Can you guess the names of these hams sandwiched in close together?

Those cool dudes of pork Greggio and Storch!

The Silence of the Hams: A Pictorial Memoir

Val (John Astin's wife), me, John and Rosey. Someone in this picture thought pasta fagioli was called Pasta for Julie.

Another cast lunch in Los Angeles. Ezio Greggio, Dom DeLuise, Charlene Tilton, me, Stuart Pankin, Dan McVicar and Rudy DeLuca. Everyone pictured has hambition.

(Top) Count Greggio. He was in Mel Brooks' *Dracula* with Leslie Nielsen.

(Bottom) Joanna Pacula and Charlene Tilton at our wrap party.

The Silence of the Hams: A Pictorial Memoir

Feel the love: Dom DeLuise, Rino Piccolo kissing my head (he played the Ambulance Driver), and Ezio Greggio. That's Joanna Stein peeking in next to Dom. Ezio ate the baby corn cob in his mouth after this picture was taken and then pulled a hamstring.

Dinner in Los Angeles, with Ezio, Mel and Rudy at Ago Restaurant in West Hollywood. Mel sang my full name "Craig Campobasso" as the red wine flowed, all night long like an Italian song. The patrons of the restaurant loved it! So did I.

PHYLLIS DILLER: THE QUEEN OF COMEDY

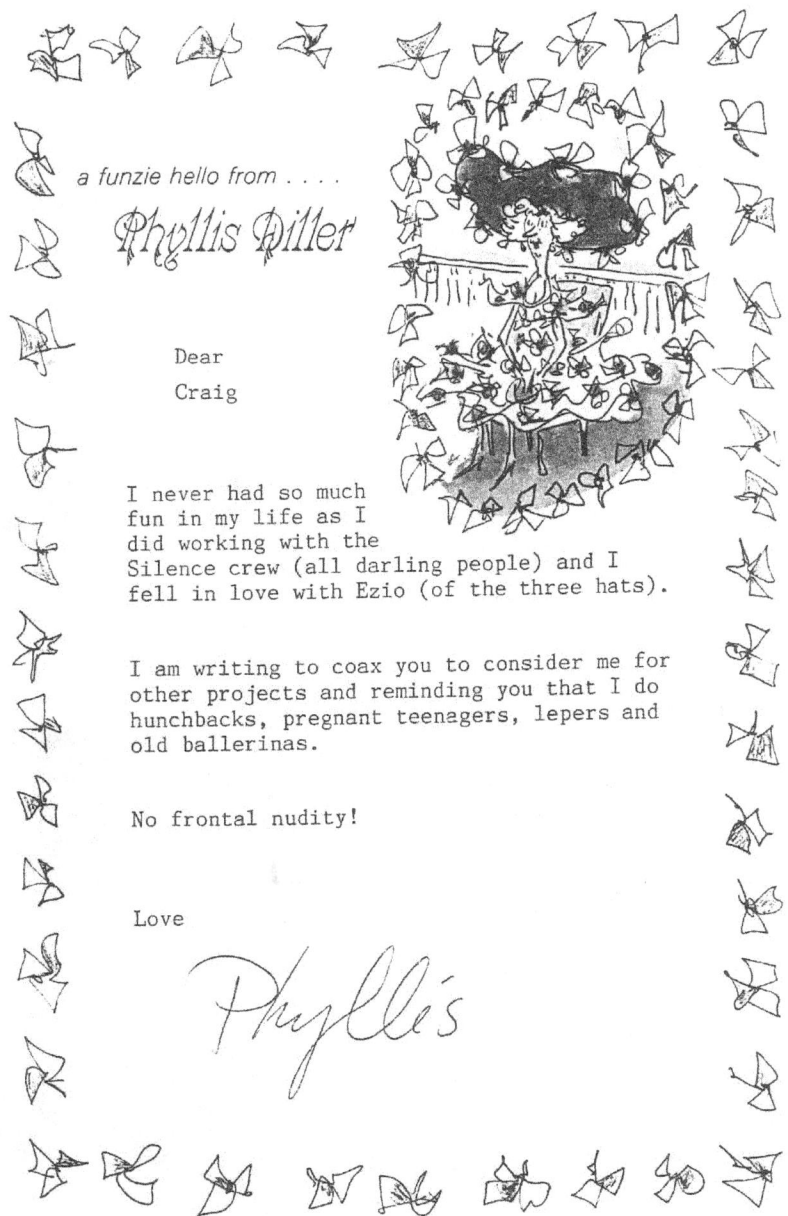

a funzie hello from . . . .

Phyllis Diller

Dear
Craig

I never had so much
fun in my life as I
did working with the
Silence crew (all darling people) and I
fell in love with Ezio (of the three hats).

I am writing to coax you to consider me for
other projects and reminding you that I do
hunchbacks, pregnant teenagers, lepers and
old ballerinas.

No frontal nudity!

Love

Phyllis

Ezio's wrote this to Phyllis Diller: EZIO GREGGIO. Milano, Italy, 1994 April 5. "Thank so much for the wonderful present I received with the funniest letter of the world. I'm very happy to know that you didn't forget me and sometimes you find the time to write me a letter. You did a great job for my little movie that has been released with good success: the Italians laugh a lot with your funny role. I hope to be in LA at the end of April or beginning of July and I will ask to our friend Craig Campobasso to arrange a dinner with you: I like to meet you and let you know of my next projects. I love you Phyllis, you're a great Actress, a great Woman, you're great. A big kiss, see you soon." (Sorry for the terrible English.)

Well dinner in 1994 turned into lunch. Ezio and I went to Phyllis Diller's house near the ocean. She drove us in her Excalibur car down Sunset Blvd, to Gladstone's on the beach. To watch every face light up when they saw Phyllis Diller is an experience in itself. Light and laughter is evoked just laying eyes on her.

Beautiful Memories with the Grande Dame of Comedy.

(Left) After lunch, I took this artsy photo of Phyllis and Ezio.

The seagull took my direction well, and flew just above Ezio's head as planned. But he wouldn't poop on cue.

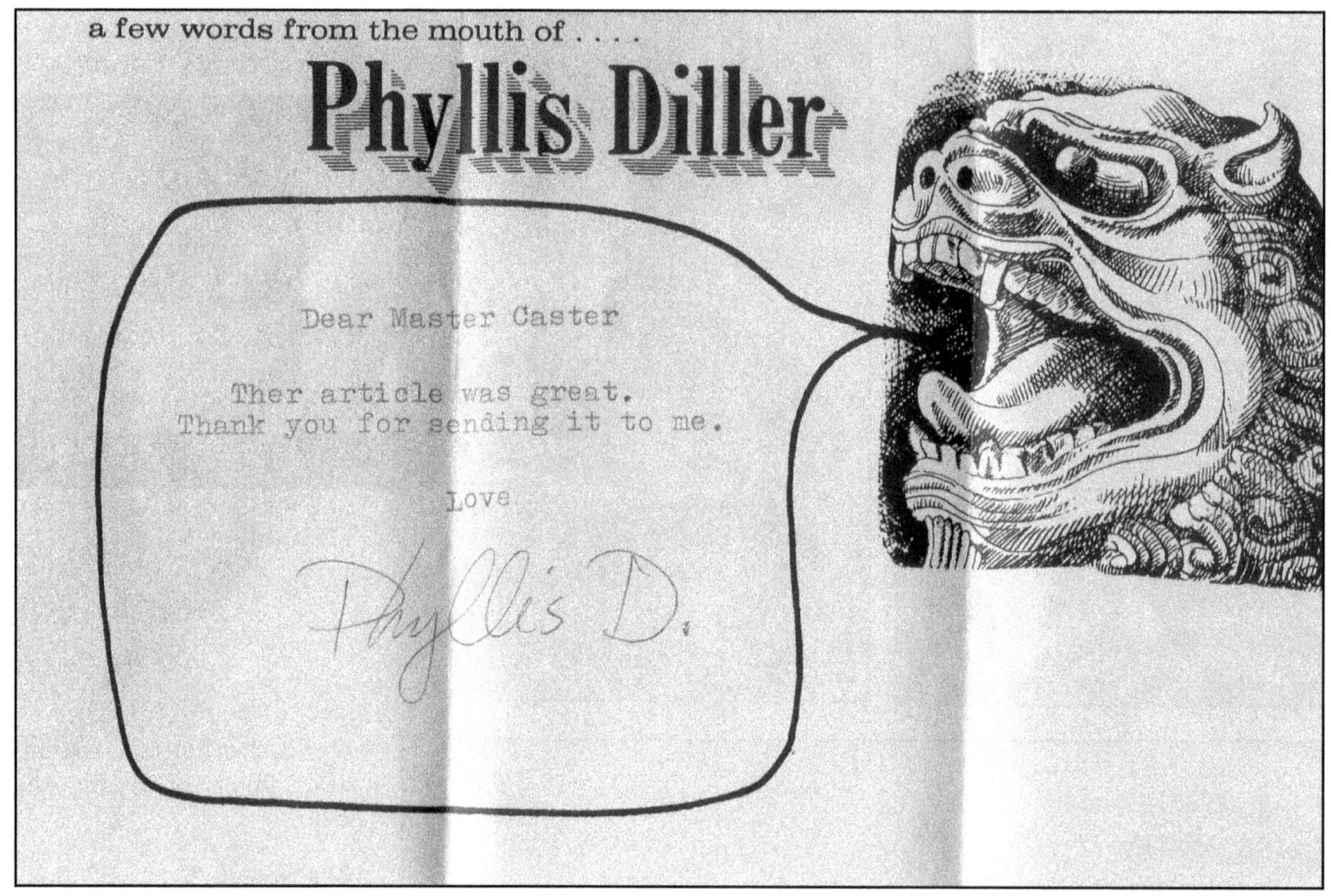

Phyllis sent this note to me after the Drama-Logue article came out where she named me The Master Caster!

Production Stills

A production still is a part of every film and is used for publicity. They are behind-the-scenes but are often posed and more formal than candid shots. This way they represent parts of the film that will capture the interest of reviewers and the audience during the launch. Here are some production stills from *The Silence of the Hams*.

Thank god they can't read or they'd be dead.

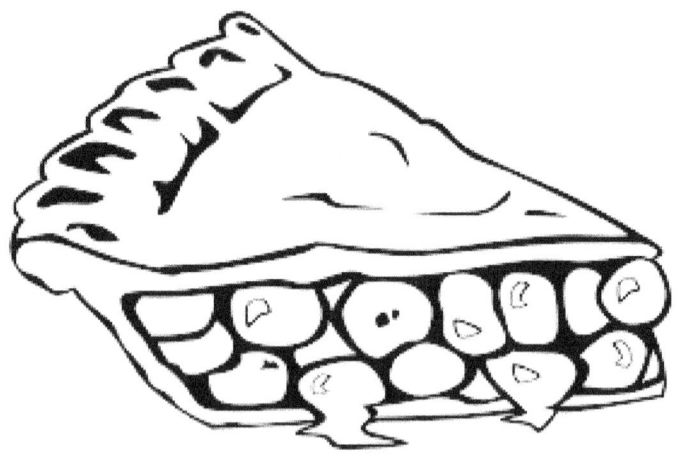

Dr. Animal liked the brains of an intellect and cherry pie.

Charlene's (Jane) wondering why a stranger is taking their picture.

Billy liked getting water dumped on him so we did it five more times just to appease him.

The Silence of the Hams: A Pictorial Memoir

(Left) "No Spitting, no barfing, no button pushing." Charlene only did one of those things. Can you guess which one?

(Middle Left) Dr. Animal's hands were tied. He couldn't make Jo a pizza. Boy was Jo mad!

(Bottom Left) Dr. Animal's mug shot. "Sometimes I get a little manic and you can't stop me. I'm all over the place. I have fun." Dom DeLuise

Detective Balsam was always searching for Jane Wine. He finally gave up and bought a bottle of wine and got drunk instead.

Opposite Page (Top) After Jane checks in to the Cemetery Motel with the stolen money she spoofs Demi Moore's *Indecent Proposal*.

(Bottom) Jane's fun is short-lived when she takes a shower and Antonio later drags her lifeless body outside.

Our Itinerary

Hotel Principe De Savoia in Milan, Italy
Sunday, February 27, 1994
Dinner with Ezio Greggio at 8:00 PM.

Monday, February 28, 1994
Free day to explore Milan.
In late afternoon, give interviews and take pictures for European Magazines.
Dinner with Ezio Greggio at 8:00 PM.

Tuesday, March 1, 1994
• In the morning give interviews and take pictures at hotel for magazines, and then television interviews.
• In the afternoon rehearsal at Studio Channel 5 for *The Ezio Greggio Show*, a 2-hour special about *The Silence of the Hams*.
• Dinner in a terrible Italian restaurant…I'm sorry…terrific restaurant. (Ezio's fun sense-of-humor spilled into our itinerary.)

Wednesday March 1, 1994
10:00 AM: Arrive at Studio Channel 5 for wardrobe and make-up for *The Ezio Greggio Show*.
1:00 PM: Tape the show.
9:00 PM: Dinner and party at Ezio's house in Milan.

The Silence of the Hams: A Pictorial Memoir

I decided to take my mother Marie on this trip with me, as she had never been out of the states. I always included my mother and father and two sisters in everything I did. Mom and Dad were extras, including my Godmother Mercy on many movies I cast. I loved seeing the joy it brought them.

We arrived in Milan on Sunday, February 27, 1994. This is a photo of us standing outside the Hotel Principe De Savoia with Marie (my Mom), Me, Rudy and Nancy DeLuca, John and Val Astin. Also on trip not pictured were: Joanna Pacula and Daniel McVicar.

Before we left on the trip, I told my Mom jokingly, wouldn't it be great if we saw Sophia Loren (one of my all-time favorite actresses) and Pope John Paul. (Well, when in Rome.)

While staying in Milan, Mom and I were having coffee in the Hotel Principe De Savoia's grand lobby. The group Duran Duran was staying at the hotel so there were many groupies hanging around to get a glimpse of the boy band. Suddenly the elevator doors opened, and as if in slow motion, Sophia Loren stepped out, elegant and glamorous. She sauntered to the front door and got into a chauffeured car and off she went. My mouth fell open. First wish granted!

(Top) While in Milan, Ezio also showed us the movie for the first time. What a treat! In the screening room: Joanna Pacula, Val and John Astin, and Rudy DeLuca.

(Bottom) *The Ezio Greggio Show* taping on March 1, 1994. That screen is set inside a giant ham. I can still hear the special's song in my head: Ezio Greggio—is the show!

(Top) The set! A whole sounder of swine walked that blue carpet.

(Left) John Astin and Joanna Pacula rehearsing.

(Top) All hams on deck: Ezio's ready to tape.

(Right) Giving Rudy a good luck kiss before he tapes, Italian style. We begged him to take a shower, but he liked the grunge look, because it was all the rage with the kids, and he wanted to fit in.

(Top) The dancing girls on the show. OO LALA!

(Bottom) We all looked like ghosts with the make-up they put on us. That's me, Matteo, Joanna, Daniel and Rudy. Getting ready for the finale when we all walk down the stairs and Ezio says something wonderful in Italian about each of us. I came out last, and Ezio talked for some time. I had no idea what he said. I asked John Astin (who spoke Italian) and he replied, "Ezio basically made you the King of Italy for the day!"

Bravo Ezio! Bravo! But I never got the crown?

(Top) Ezio getting ready to descend the stairs for the finale!

(Bottom) Dinner at Ezio's the night of the taping. Leslie Nielson gave Ezio one of his famous fart contraptions that he handmade and depending how you squeezed it in your hand, would make different sounding (long or short) farts. It was a source of laughter all night long. Nancy, Craig, Marie, Val, John, Isabel, Matteo and Rudy at the House of Flatulence.

The Silence of the Hams: A Pictorial Memoir

Our gracious hosts: Ezio and Isabel.

(Top) The night of Ezio's dinner party he unveiled the new *Hams* poster for the states. Upon first seeing it, we all laughed out loud. We signed each other's posters that night.

Roma

Our Itinerary
De La Ville Inter-Continental Hotel in Roma, Italy

Thursday, March 3, 1994
10:00 AM: Fly to Rome. (50 minute flight)
11:00 AM: Transfer from airport and check into hotel.
1:00 PM: Press conference with journalists.
7:00 PM: Cast on Italian talk show.
10:00 PM: Dinner in a wonderful Italian restaurant

Friday and Saturday, March 4 & 5, 1994
Free days to explore Roma!

On a free day in Rome, Mom and I went to the Vatican and Sistine Chapel with Val Astin. John was not feeling well and opted to rest at the hotel. After viewing the Pietà sculpture by Michelangelo, I heard music coming from the front of the church, so Mom and I went to investigate. Pope John Paul was walking in procession to give a rare mass.

It was as if the heaven's heard me and granted my second wish.

An illustration of the Pietà.

ROMA! Mama Marie and me outside the Vatican. A gorgeous color prism splayed up and down Mom's body; a happy sign of things to come.

(Top) Shh! *Il Silenzio dei Prosciutti* press conference has begun.

(Bottom) Hams cutting Prosciutti!

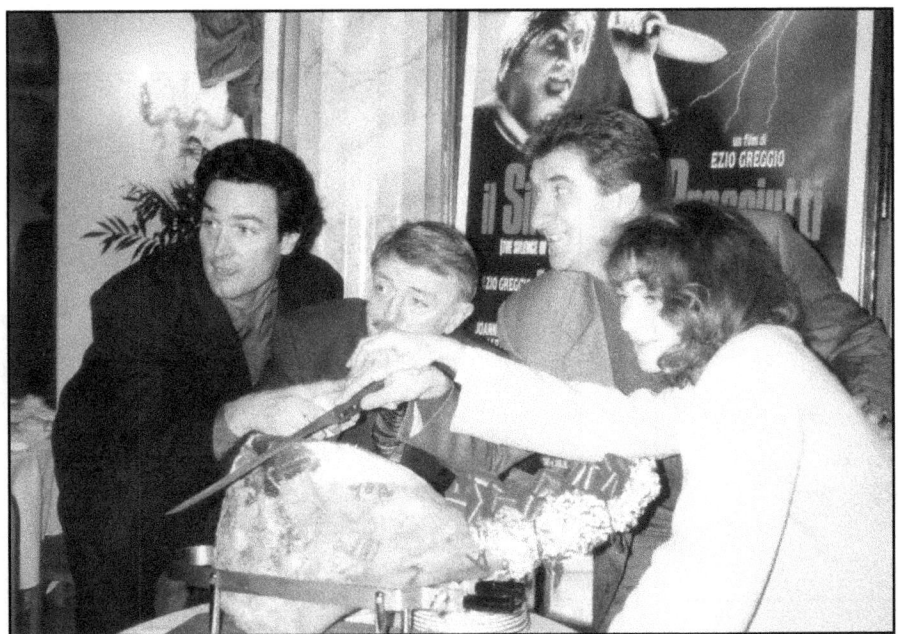

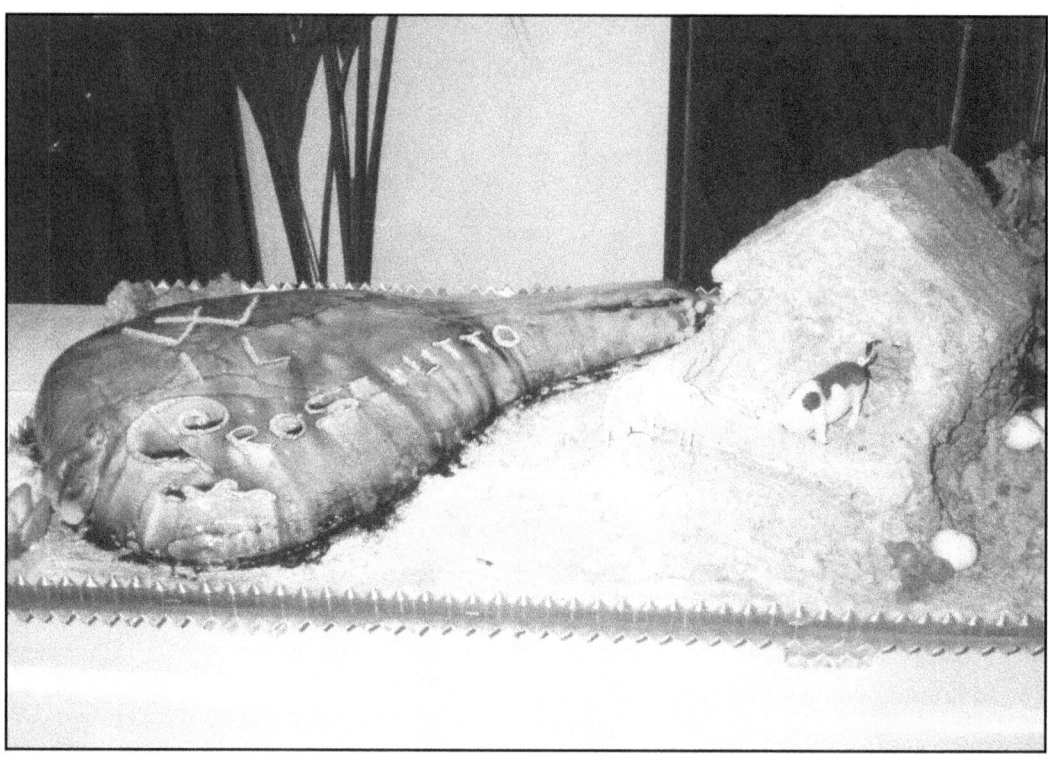

(Top) The press ate up the laughter and the cake!

(Bottom) One more gratuitous shot of our ham-burglars.

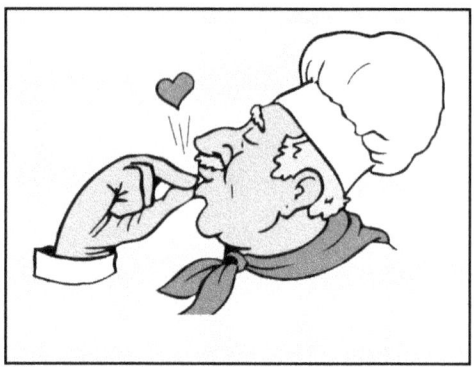

(Bottom) Now it's time to play in Rome. Tossing coins and making wishes in the most famous fountain in the world The Trevi Fountain. Throughout my life, every time a wish was to be had, I would ask Mom what she wished for. Her answer was always the same: "I wished that your wish would come true."

(Above) Another day we went the famous coliseum. Marie, John and Val.

(Right) While at the coliseum, fans spotted John Astin. Because of the language barrier, they kept repeating, "Da Da Da Dum (Snap Snap) over and over. John graciously took pictures with them and signed autographs.

(Bottom Left) A before dinner shot at hotel with Marie and Joanna.

(Bottom Right) Getting ready to go out on the town for dinner! What a spiffy looking bunch. No one ate ham.

A great meal was had by all! After dinner, Ezio walked us through the elegant streets of Rome and we went to Vatican City to see it all lit up at night. It was beautiful and magical. Everything was bathed in gold light.

Vatican City

FAX

TO: CRAIG CAMPOBASSO (THE BEST)

PGS:1

Milan May 12, 1994

Dear Craig,
first of all ...I love You! I hope that's all ok for you and Mamy. In a few days I'll be in LA. I let you know exactly the date of my arrival that I suppose it will be around May 19 or 20.

I sent you today a letter with a copy of the remboursement done from Hotel Principi di Savoia for John Astin in April 13. I hope that he has already received it , in other case let me know.

I'm going to Cannes film market to meet the Spanish, German and France distributors.

Please tell to my Agents...sorry our Agents that I will be soon in town to organize some meetings.

A big kiss, say hello to everybody when you talk with the friends, see you soon, I miss you

Ciao!

GUESS WHO ARE THEY?

A New Generation of Ham's Fans with the Blu-Ray Release

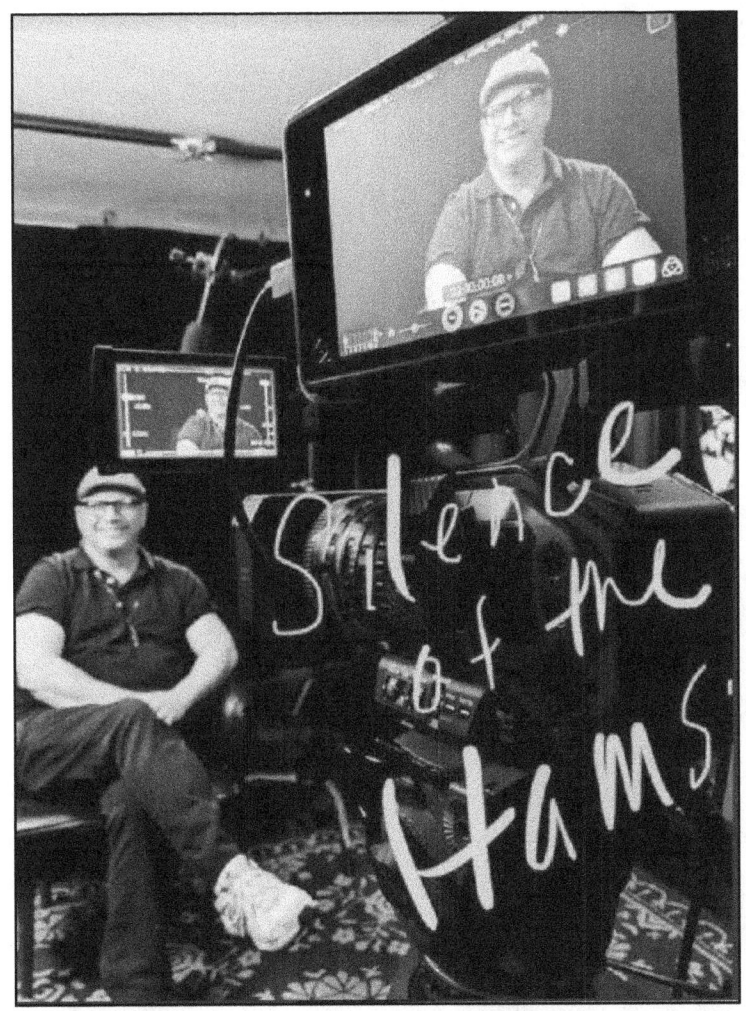

(Left) On Friday, February 1, 2019, I was interviewed for the 25th Anniversary Blu-ray rerelease for *The Silence of the Hams*. Be sure and get your copy to see our cast and crew interviews and commentary watching the film.

(Right) In October of 2019 the big ham & cheese himself was interviewed for the behind-the-scenes documentary for the Blu-ray rerelease at Mr. C Hotel in Beverly Hills.

The night of October 19, 2019, Ezio, Charlene, Billy and I recorded the commentary for the Blu-ray rerelease. Jim Kunz (pictured far left) was the documentary's cast and crew videographer.

(Top) Hammies in the recording studio giving commentary.

(Bottom) I told them to act natural. Look what happened.

To top the evening off we ate a late dinner at L'Atica Pizzeria Da Michele in Hollywood, CA. Francesco Zimone, the owner brought us all bite size portions of every pasta dish and samplers of their famous pizzas. We were in pig heaven. Sitting next to Ezio is Italian actress Romina Pierdomenico. They star in the hit Italian TV show *La sai l'ultima*.

Parting Oinks

(Top) Charlene today as she appeared in the documentary.

(Bottom) Charlene on her audition day.

CHARLENE TILTON

MY SET STORIES

The entire cast and crew of *The Silence of the Hams* became a family and we had the best time under the charge of our fearless leader Ezio. When you have comic geniuses like Dom DeLuise and Phyllis Diller of course laughs were plentiful.

One day Phyllis and I were in the make-up trailer getting ready for our next scenes. Phyllis had so much plastic surgery and she always talked about it in her act. She looked beautiful so the makeup lady had to paint wrinkles on her face to make her look older. I was being fitted for shoes to wear on my knees to make me look shorter for a sight gag. I looked over at Phyllis and said, "Only in Hollywood would they be making you look older and me shorter." She laughed so hard.

My favorite memory is filming a song and dance number to the Italian song "Funiculì, Funiculà." Ezio and I worked so hard on that but it didn't make it in the final cut of the movie. Hopefully they added it into the Blu-ray rerelease.

(Top) Saying goodbye is such sweet-and-sour pork.

(Bottom) Ezio and my Mom Marie. Yes, I let her adopt him, so I could have brother from another mother.

Billy got a parting gift from the cast and crew. We all signed Jo's boxer shorts. Photo courtesy: Matteo Molinari. Then Billy gave Ezio a parting gift too! A pie in the ole kisser!

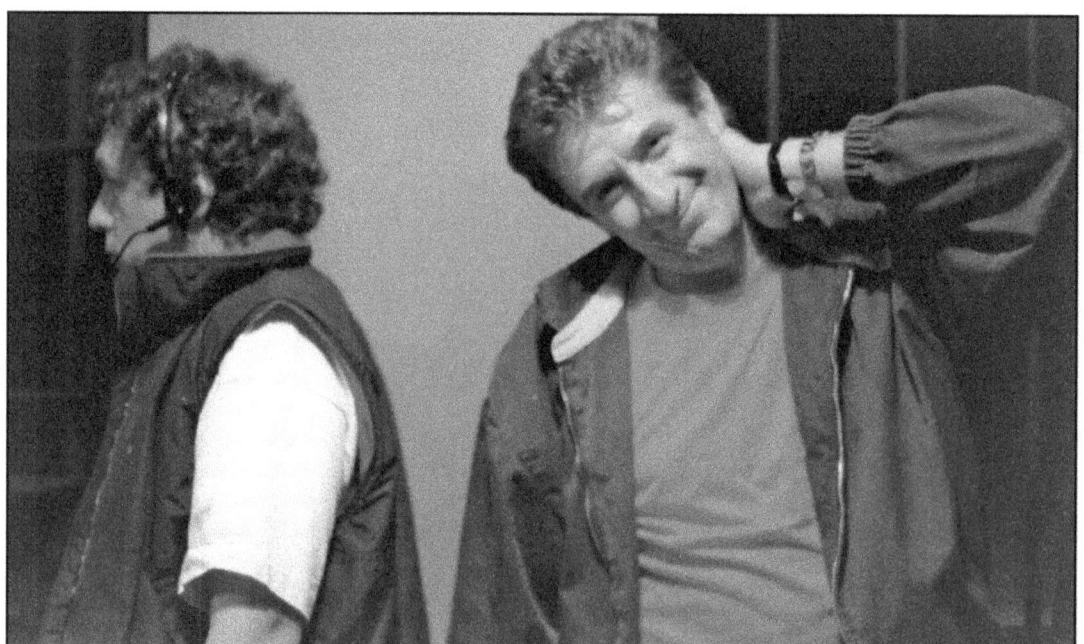

(Top) I'll leave you with this picture of Ezio. No matter the long hours on set, there was always a smile on his face. I hope you'll smile too after looking at all the good times we had on this production.

Photo courtesy: Matteo Molinari.

Original Hammy promotion. Love the canned ham.

About the Author: CRAIG CAMPOBASSO

Multiple award-winning filmmaker and Emmy-nominated casting director Craig Campobasso was fifteen when he started in the entertainment business. His young acting career was off to a great start; he landed his first national commercial for McDonald's chicken sandwich, and spoke his first line of dialogue to Tuesday Weld in a MOW.

After graduating high school at age seventeen, Craig went to work behind-the-scenes on such blockbuster film classics as Frank Herbert's *Dune* directed by David Lynch; and two Arnold Schwarzenegger movies *Conan The Destroyer* and *Total Recall*. He began his casting career on Steven Spielberg's *Amazing Stories*. He received an Emmy nomination for Outstanding Casting for a Series on David E. Kelley's *Picket Fences*. Craig's casting career spans three decades, including films like *Sky Captain and the World of Tomorrow* starring Jude Law and Angelina Jolie, *Prancer* starring Sam Elliott, *The Silence of the Hams* starring Ezio Greggio and Dom DeLuise, *The Godson* starring Rodney Dangerfield and Dom DeLuise, *Don't Come Back from the Moon* starring James Franco and Rashida Jones, and recently *Starbright* starring Diego Boneta and John Rhys-Davies.

Craig's mother Marie Donna King Campobasso told him from the time she was pregnant with him, that she knew he would become a writer. He fulfilled that prophecy when he was twenty-six, after he experienced a life-changing spiritual awakening. That's when *The Autobiography of an ExtraTerrrestrial Saga* book series was born. There are four installments of the series at present that will expand to seven volumes. Craig's latest book *The Extraterrestrial Species Almanac: The Ultimate Guide to Greys, Reptilians, Hybrids, and Nordics* will be released January 1, 2020. His passion is to write stories that provoke the reader to think, to raise their consciousness, to expand their mind about Creation, while still entertaining in the Hollywood tradition.

Craig directed, wrote and produced the short film *Stranger at the Pentagon*, which was adapted from the popular UFO book authored by the late Dr. Frank E. Stranges. After production, the short film collected accolades. In September 2014, it won Best Sci-Fi film at the Burbank International Film Festival, selling out all 275 seats—a first for the festival. In 2015, it won a Remi Award at the Worldfest Houston International Film Festival for Best Sci-Fi Short.

Craig has appeared on many radio shows, including several appearances on *Coast to Coast AM* with George Noory. He has also been a guest on the *Open Minds* talk show, with Regina Meredith; and an episode of *Beyond Belief*, hosted by George Noory on www.Gaia.com. Craig has also appeared on The History Channel's *Ancient Aliens*.

To learn more about Craig Campobasso go to:
www.CraigCampobasso.com
or
www.AutobiographyOfAnET.com
or
www.StrangerAtThePentagon.com

Facebook
Craig Campobasso
Craig Campobasso Casting
The Autobiography of an ExtraTerrestrial *Saga*
Stranger at the Pentagon

Twitter
@CraigCampobasso
@ThyronBooks
@PentagonThor

Instagram
@Craig_Campobasso
@ThyronBooks
@StrangerAtThePentagon

SNIPPET FROM
THE GREAT LIFE (HOLLYWOOD REPORTER) BY GEORGE CHRISTY JUNE 4, 1993

At first, it was to be a spoof of Alfred Hitchcock's classic thriller, *Psycho*, in which Tony Perkins played Norman Bates the murderer as well as his mother, but then Italian comedian Ezio Greggio saw *The Silence of the Lambs*, loved it and decided to incorporate some of those characters in the spoof, which he now calls *The Silence of the Hams,* with Dom DeLuise playing Dr. Animal (a takeoff of Hannibal Lecter), Billy Zane as Joe Dee Fostar (Jodie Foster role), Charlene Tilton and Joanna Pacula playing sisters, Shelley Winters as Tony Perkin's mother from *Psycho,* along with Mel Brooks and Anne Bancroft in cameos. John Astin, Phyllis Diller, Martin Balsam, John Landis, Larry Storch, Rip Taylor, *The Bold and the Beautiful's* Dan McVicar, Rudy DeLuca, Henry Silva, Rosey Brown, Bubba Smith, Nedra Volz. Quite a roundup of actors, thanks to casting director Craig Campobasso, who joined Ezio and the evening's host Bob Kovoloff (a product placement whiz) and numerous cast members at the San Remo ("Italian Restaurant and Pizza") in Van Nuys to celebrate the completion of the shooting *Note Anne Bancroft did not appear in the picture. She only visited the set.

Finally the cast is looking in the same direction. (Don't tell Shelley.)

SNIPPET FROM DRAMA-LOGUE May 27-June 2, 1993

"Stars on the Set with Their "Master Caster" CRAIG CAMPOBASSO Breaking the "Silence of the Hams"

By Elias Stimac

The dark and dusty passageway leads to a shadowy basement filled with macabre cobwebs, mysterious characters, and…movie cameras? Also lurking in the shadows are legendary actress Shelley Winters, director Ezio Greggio, producer Julie Corman, and dozens of crew people. Actually, they are working on a scene from their psycho-illogical thriller spoof, *The Silence of the Hams*. And at a safe distance, happily watching the scary film, is casting director Craig Campobasso, enjoying the fruits of his pre-production labor.

Producer Corman is in awe of Campobasso's results. "I have three Ds about Craig: the first is he's dedicated, the second is he's directed, and the third one is he delivers—I mean, whatever you need, he delivers it. He loves actors so much, he creates an aura that makes them comfortable, so they all want to come and be in your movie."

Always bubbling with intensity and wit, Dom DeLuise takes a moment to give his views on how Campobasso put together the ensemble. "When I spoke to Craig about doing this movie, he reminded me of all the actors already committed to the picture and how he put them together. I really respect what he does—he has to be so aware of the acting community. He's very present, having all those names and those repertories in his head. Also, I don't think it's an easy job to cast a satirical movie—you need to find people who will do the best job when it comes to satire."

Funnywoman Phyllis Diller had some serious praise for the casting director. "The most important thing in a movie is the casting of the characters. And if there was ever a master of this fine art, it is Craig Campobasso. He truly gets inside people and feels their talent in an almost psychic way. He's a master caster!"

Epilogue

When I was a teenager I sat in movie theaters and watched Mel Brooks movies. I dreamt of working with the King of Comedy someday. I loved spoof movies! …including the *Airplane* and *Naked Gun* franchises. Back then I wanted to be an actor because I wanted to be in satirical films such as those.

Just out of high school an opportunity arose for me to work behind the scenes on *Dune* and *Conan the Destroyer*. I jumped at the chance. That gig lasted four years. I soaked in everything about the film business during those formative years. At age twenty-three I went into casting and discovered I had a talent for it. So I gave up trying to become an actor. I was a people person, a terrific liaison between talent and production, agents and managers. I also loved actors and their process of discovering the character. Over time I became an acting teacher as well.

Some of my favorite comedians besides Mel Brooks were Burt Reynolds, Dom DeLuise, Phyllis Diller and Larry Storch. Little did I know when I was a kid that my dream of working with these movie greats would come true. Although Burt was not in *Hams*, I worked with him on a few other projects, the last feature called *Forget About It* opposite Raquel Welch.

When setting up a film at the major talent agencies who handle star names, I send them the script, and then discuss who they have that might fit into our budget and timeframe. Once I set the first star, I call or e-mail every agency to inform them. This gets an excitement rolling within the agencies. As more stars are cast, the agencies just want their clients in the film and start offering up more and more ideas.

Dom DeLuise did extensive preparation for his role and came to set with props and improv. Every take was different, hilarious and unique. Not only was Dom well prepared, but Billy Zane was too. It's not an easy task keep up with the master. Billy enjoyed the freedom to explore every take with Dom, to let go, and have fun. Once I set Dom's and Billy's deals, academy award winning actors Shelley Winters and Martin Balsam joined the cast, and the rest fell into place. Once Mel Brooks was game to do a cameo, other star names were begging for cameos just to join in on the crazy fun. To work with the greatest comedians of all time happens only once in a lifetime. You have to grab the opportunity for it to be recorded on celluloid forever.

People ask me what it was like working with all these legends. It was like being locked in a wonderful warp of time, where I wished we all had more time together. It was a realm where all things were funny. I never wanted to leave the set. When I look back on the experience, it's like a dream sequence in a movie that happened in reality once upon a time. All I am left with is smiles, love, laughter and lasting friendships.

I hope you have enjoyed this pictorial memoir and learned about the making of *The Silence of the Hams*. It was a great joy and honor to work on this hilarious movie. We all need a little silliness in life. Pop the Blu-ray rerelease of our beloved cult classic into your player and watch the documentary, commentary of Ezio, Charlene, Billy and me watching the film, and of course a remastered color version that will tickle your funny bone.

I'll be seeing you in the movies.

In Memoriam

In the twenty-five years since the film's release we've sadly lost these members of our cast.

Dom DeLuise (1933–2009)

Phyllis Diller (1917–2012)

Martin Balsam (1919–1996)

Bubba Smith (1945–2011)

Rip Taylor (1931–2019)

Shelley Winters (1920–2006)

Nedra Volz (1908–2003)

Andre Rosey Brown (1956–2006)

Irwin Keyes (1952–2015)

Al Ruscio (1924–2013)

Wilhelm von Homburg (1940–2004)

www.ingramcontent.com/pod-product-compliance
Lightning Source LLC
Chambersburg PA
CBHW081839170426
43199CB00017B/2777